Wedding Style

Wedding Style

*hundreds of tips and secrets from the
professionals for styling your own big day*

Carole Hamilton
with photographs by Rodney Bailey

RYLAND
PETERS
& SMALL

LONDON NEW YORK

Designer Liz Sephton
Senior Editor Henrietta Heald
Picture Research Carole Hamilton
Production Gemma John
Art Director Leslie Harrington
Publishing Director Alison Starling

First published in the United Kingdom in
2009 by Ryland Peters & Small
20–21 Jockey's Fields
London WC1R 4BW
and
First published in the United States in
2009
by Ryland Peters & Small Inc.
519 Broadway, 5th Floor
New York, NY 10012
www.rylandpeters.com

10 9 8 7 6 5 4 3 2 1

Text © copyright Carole Hamilton 2009
Design copyright © Ryland Peters & Small
2009

All commissioned photography © Ryland
Peters & Small. See acknowledgements
page 160 for further copyright information.

ISBN: 978-1-84597-762-7

A CIP record of this book is available from the
British Library.

Library of Congress Cataloging-in-Publication
Data

Hamilton, Carole.
  Wedding style : hundreds of tips and secrets
from the professionals for styling your own big
day / Carole Hamilton ; with photographs by
Rodney Bailey.
      p. cm.
  Includes index.
  ISBN 978-1-84597-762-7
  1. Weddings--Planning. I. Title.
  HQ745.H236 2009
  395.2'2--dc22

2008018361

Printed in China

contents

introduction

I have been involved in the wedding industry for over 15 years, both as a magazine editor and while researching several books on the subject, so it's a topic very close to my heart. In that time I have marvelled at the way so many couples have been able to bring a touch of uniqueness to their very special day. Managing to create a magical event without a huge budget, adding personal touches that speak volumes about them as a couple and making the whole celebration so much more meaningful for them and their guests.

Weddings are not about money but about style – and that is what this book is all about. Working with the cash you do have to create a day that's all your own. It is about having the ability to stamp your personalities on everything from the stationery to the finishing touches on a spectacular cake. The introduction of details that reflect your lives, mixed with ideas borrowed from both your family's heritage as well as a dash of well-loved bridal traditions.

Styling a beautiful wedding sounds daunting and you may think you're not creative enough to bring it all together. But with a little help, I think every couple has it in them to create an amazing event, quite simply because it is your day and only you know what it will take to realise the dream.

Here are my top three tips to guide you as you begin your quest for wedding perfection:

Never underestimate the value of teamwork. In the run-up to your wedding you will be hiring a host of professionals eager to help you fulfil your dream. This 'dream team' (that also includes family and friends) needs to understand exactly how you see every minute of the day, so it is important to brief them well. Creating a mood board is invaluable. It is not always easy to articulate what's inside your head but showing a selection of pictures, fabric swatches and colour ideas instantly makes your vision so much easier to understand.

Plan like a professional. Weddings are a lot of hard work but providing you are organised, you should make it up the aisle smiling. Make all your key decisions as soon as you can, and then stick to them. Start a wedding file, confirm everything in writing and keep copies of all correspondence. And make sure you open a bridal bank account.

Keep it all in perspective. The most important part of your wedding day is marrying the person you love – everything else is just the icing on the cake. Yes, you want your guests to be wowed by all your clever ideas – the gorgeous flowers, the delicious menu – and come away having enjoyed a wonderful occasion. But ultimately, every wedding is about the coming together of two people and the joining of two families. Long after your colour co-ordinated confetti has been swept away, all everyone will actually remember are your happy, smiling faces.

Enjoy the book and I hope it inspires you to plan your own beautiful wedding.

Carole Hamilton

capturing your vision

The perfect wedding is an occasion
filled with love and laughter – wonderful
memories-in-the-making for the happy
couple and all their guests. It should
also be a day that says something about
the bride and groom, a coming together
of ideas that reflects their personalities
and speaks volumes about their
individual tastes and style.

capturing your vision

Close your eyes and imagine just what your perfect wedding would look like. Is the setting a fairytale castle, a sunny garden, a contemporary loft or a sandy beach? Whatever your dream, this vision is the starting point for your big day. It will probably have been inspired by the time of year when the wedding is due to take place, the style of venue, or a favourite colour or flower.

Every couple is different, and each wedding is a highly personal event. It is hard to generalize about weddings, and there are no right or wrong choices. One couple may happily spend thousands on a lavish reception, while another will prefer to spend their budget on a more intimate party and a once-in-a-lifetime honeymoon. It is your wedding and your budget to spend in any way you want in order to create those all-important memories.

So where do you begin in the quest for the perfect wedding? The important thing is not to panic. In the whirlwind of excitement surrounding any engagement, it is easy to make hasty decisions that you could later regret once the picture of your ideal day becomes clearer. Successful planning depends on being well organized, so at the earliest opportunity make a file for storing appointment cards, magazine cuttings, supplier confirmations and receipts. Computer-savvy brides may like to create a budget spreadsheet and online 'to do' list, but it is advisable to have a folder for paperwork. Once you have set up a file, you can start to think about how your ideal day will look and feel.

Set aside time to investigate what's available in your area that falls within your budget. Most venues and companies are prepared to accept provisional bookings on the proviso that you confirm by an agreed date. Listen to advice from family and friends, but don't be swayed into changing your ideas to keep someone else happy – you'll almost always end up regretting it.

The most successful weddings are those that reflect the individual personalities and flair of the bride and groom. If you want to discover what will make your dream complete, start by listing your and your partner's wedding priorities. You may think that everything is equally important, but when budget dictates that your wildest fantasies may not be affordable, it's as well to know early on what is essential and what belongs on the wish list.

TOP At an outdoor wedding, brightly coloured fabric runners are used to link the chairs and to frame the ceremony location.

ABOVE Including children in your ceremony celebrates the family element in marriage.

trade secret

'Most brides have dreamed about their wedding day for years so, when the time comes, they know where they want to start. I always tell my brides to go with their heart. I think personal taste is more important than what's trendy. Brides are allowed to break the rules!'

Preston Bailey, wedding and event designer

Your wedding is about you and your fiancé, so the initial planning decisions should be made by the two of you together. It is important that you share the same vision and, if necessary, agree to compromise so that you end up with a day that feels special to you both.

Make a list of all the elements that you want to form part of your day and then divide the items in the list into 'must-haves' and 'non-essential extras'. As well as beginning to build up a clearer picture of what's important, the list will be invaluable when it comes to apportioning the budget.

my ideal wedding is:

▢ formal
▢ semi-formal
▢ casual

I want the overall style to be:

▢ elegant and traditional
▢ themed
▢ casual and fun

I want to invite:

▢ just close family and friends
▢ 75–100 guests
▢ over 100 guests

I want the reception to be:

▢ a seated meal followed by dancing
▢ a buffet, barbecue or picnic
▢ a cocktail party with canapés

wedding priorities

Use this list to obtain a clearer picture of what matters most on your big day. Rank the items in order of importance to create your ultimate list.

✶ atmosphere
✶ bridal gown
✶ bridesmaids
✶ cake
✶ decoration
✶ favours
✶ flowers
✶ food
✶ honeymoon
✶ location/venue
✶ music and entertainment
✶ number of guests
✶ photography
✶ stationery
✶ transport
✶ video
✶ wine

TOP Create a focal point at the entrance to your reception. An impressive flower arrangement or stylishly designed table plan both work well.

ABOVE Centrepieces should be tall enough to let guests see one another across the table.

RIGHT If the chairs at your venue are mismatched, consider hiring chair covers. These are available in plenty of colours but cream often works best. You can then select coloured sashes to match your theme and finish with an attractive touch such as the addition of a fresh flower.

DEFINING YOUR STYLE

When you talk to other people about your plans, you will probably be asked, more than once, what is your wedding style? Rather than being something to worry about, style simply means the image that you have in your head of the day, in particular how it looks and feels. And you are probably closer to setting a style than you think, since the choices you have made about location, colour, flowers and atmosphere will come together to give the day a style label that is instantly recognizable to others. Your wedding style can be pretty much anything – from traditional to contemporary, from romantic to fun, from formal to downright quirky.

traditional

The most traditional style of wedding consists of a ceremony followed by a drinks reception, a seated meal in the late afternoon or early evening, and then a party with dancing.
pros You can spend the whole day with friends and family. Suits both religious and civil ceremonies.
cons Usually the most expensive option.

informal

A typical informal occasion is likely to involve a civil ceremony followed by a buffet-style reception or cocktail party in the afternoon, with guests usually departing in the late afternoon.
pros A cost-effective option that will suit couples who want to avoid unnecessary fuss.
cons You may feel that the occasion was all over very quickly – and that you would have preferred a little more fuss!

the wedding weekend

This is a popular formula that involves a limited number of guests arriving at a venue on a Friday; the ceremony takes place on the Saturday followed by a formal reception, then everyone meets up again on the Sunday for breakfast before leaving.
pros A wonderfully indulgent way of celebrating with close family and friends.
cons Expensive. Since the venues offering this service tend to be smaller than the alternatives, the number of guests will necessarily be limited.

BELOW A vibrant colour scheme does much to brighten up a winter reception. Votive candles can be used to highlight a pretty centrepiece.

BELOW LEFT The joining of two families and two cultures is celebrated at a beautiful red-and-white-themed Anglo-Indian wedding ceremony.

the wedding abroad

A wedding in a foreign country is a good choice for couples marrying for the second time or for anyone who wants minimal fuss and an endless choice of locations, from beaches to Italian palaces.

pros A relaxed, informal setting that can be much cheaper than a traditional wedding.

cons Some friends won't be able to join you on account of financial and time constraints.

something different

There is nothing to say that your wedding must conform to anyone else's traditions. If it suits your personalities, how about a Wild West barbecue, a Halloween-themed ghost party, or simply inviting everyone down to the local bistro for a burger?

pros Ideal for the couple who don't like the formalities and want a light-hearted occasion.

cons Some of your guests will think you are a little strange, and you may live to regret not having some traditional wedding shots for your album.

still in a quandary?

If you are still unsure about what's right for you, it's time to take a tip from the professionals and create a mood board. This is one of the first things you are likely to be asked to do if you use the services of a wedding planner – and it is a great thing for every couple to do at home in order to get a clearer picture of what their dream day looks like.

a themed wedding

Give your wedding a very personal theme based on something that interests you or your partner. Make sure the theme is reflected at all key moments throughout the day.

✳ **love of travel** Name the reception tables after places you have visited together. Paris and Venice sound so much more romantic than tables 1 and 2.

✳ **love of the movies** Name the tables after famous screen lovers, play a silent movie during dinner and put directors' chairs in the cocktail area. You could even hold the reception in a cinema.

✳ **love of sport** If either of you has a sporting passion, think about hiring an appropriate venue such as a football ground, racecourse, golf club or bowling alley.

✳ **love of flowers** A floral theme always looks beautiful and works well all year round. Use flowers decoratively at the ceremony venue, name each table after a flower and have centrepieces made to match the theme.

trade secret

'It can be incredibly daunting when you start to plan a wedding. Whether the issue is invitations, venues, flowers or colours, there is so much choice! Start by deciding what style of wedding you want – black-tie sit-down meal, barefoot beach buffet, glam cocktail party? This will help determine the general direction; you are unlikely to need a castle venue if you favour a beach buffet!'

Kathryn Lloyd, wedding designer

ABOVE Styling is all about the details. For a themed wedding, make sure everything from the stationery to the tables reflects the theme in some way. Intended for a beach celebration, this cake has rough icing to look like sand and is decorated with sugar starfish and shells.

RIGHT A summer marquee can look stark; using coloured linens is a stylish way to add a splash of colour. Here the blue tablecloths have a swirled gold pattern that is echoed in the gold chairs and gold chargers. Each napkin has been topped with a golden yellow flower.

THE WEDDING MOOD BOARD

Think about all the things you like that could possibly play a part in your wedding. Cut out pictures from magazines, explore the internet for inspirational images from other people's weddings, collect swatches of fabric and ribbon, look through flower catalogues, select your favourite colours from a paint chart, and find lettering styles from old invitations or books.

Once you have assembled a variety of items, stick them all, randomly arranged, onto a large piece of card. Sit back and look carefully at what you have created. The chances are that a definite style will start to emerge. Can you see a colour theme? Is the overall feel quite classic or does it have a more modern look? Are you favouring a particular type of venue or time of year?

This mood board will be useful when you meet any of your key suppliers such as the venue manager, the florist and the photographer. It will instantly tell them more about the type of day you want and how you see yourself. It is often difficult to put into words what's inside your head, whereas a picture can immediately make your vision crystal clear to others.

where to find inspiration

Look for ideas for your mood board from obvious and more unusual sources.

* parents' photo album
* wedding magazines
* wallpaper samples
* old movie stills
* venue websites
* food magazines
* flower catalogues
* paint colour charts
* newspaper colour supplements
* haberdashery/notions departments
* stationery sample books
* jumble and yard sales for fabric swatches

SETTING THE DATE

The time of year will undoubtedly influence the style of your wedding. In the northern hemisphere, the most popular wedding season is from June to September, for the obvious reason that the weather is likely to be better during that period, although there is an increasing trend for couples to choose the chilly delights of the winter months.

Each season has merits, but there is a great deal to be said for avoiding summer if you want to make your budget go further. Popular venues and suppliers often get booked up months, sometimes years, in advance but are quiet in early spring and autumn/fall, which will give you the opportunity to do a deal. In the same way, if you can arrange to hold your wedding on a week day, you'll probably be able to save money and to book the more sought-after suppliers, even at short notice in the summer, because they are much less likely to be busy.

Traditional times of celebration such as Easter, Thanksgiving, Christmas and Valentine's Day are also popular for weddings. Choosing a date that coincides with a wider celebration is a lovely idea but, as with the high summer months, lots of other couples will have had the same thought and you may find venues booked and others charging a premium for their services. A less expensive option would be to organize your nuptials to coincide with a landmark birthday or anniversary – perhaps marrying on the same date as your parents – and transform the day into a double celebration.

Sending out a save-the-date card is a good idea, especially if you are marrying close to holiday time, when your guests may be making their own plans.

ABOVE If your budget doesn't stretch to floral centrepieces, make a splash with brightly hued orchids on a windowsill.

BELOW A tower of individual cupcakes set on a brilliant pink tablecloth provides the focal point of this summer reception.

seasonal highlights

spring
* scented spring flowers
* pink and white blossom
* new season's fruit and vegetables
* colour palette: pink, lemon, baby blue, lime green

summer
* summer sunshine
* longer evenings
* picnics and barbeques
* colour palette: white, sunshine yellow, sky blue

autumn/fall
* crisp autumnal weather
* a riot of colour in the trees
* Thanksgiving, Halloween
* colour palette: orange, russet, green, purple, gold

winter
* Cosy log fires
* hearty menus and mulled wine
* the festive season
* colour palette: ice white, silver, green, vibrant red

trade secret

'Taste and consistency are inexpensive. All too often, people get carried away with the detail, which can result in a lack of consistency. See your wedding as if you were a guest. It's not about what you don't have; it's about what you do have and how you present it. Don't worry about fashion. Weddings are timeless and good taste is always in fashion.'

Deborah Dwek,
wedding planner

OPPOSITE The 'wow' factor at this reception comes from the use of tall vases of purple foliage dotted with lime-green orchids. The vases are wrapped in red chiffon to match the red wine glasses.

THE WEDDING BUDGET

A stylish wedding by no means depends on having a big budget. It is much more important that you use what money you have in the most productive ways. Some of the most successful weddings are impressive because of the attention that has been paid to detail and personal touches rather than because of a lavish location or exceptional food and wines, but all couples need to be aware of the size of their wedding fund before taking any major steps such as deciding on the number of guests to invite or booking a venue.

Getting married is an expensive business, with even a simple ceremony and intimate reception adding up to a substantial sum. To make sure you get your calculations right, add together everything you have saved plus a realistic amount that you think you can save during your engagement. In bygone days, the bride's father would have been expected to pay the majority of the expenses, but at a modern wedding it is much more likely to be a family affair, with the bride and groom and both sets of parents contributing to the budget.

Have the conversation about money with your parents before making any decisions that would be hard to change. It is unwise to assume anything since you may not be fully aware of their financial circumstances. Once you have discovered how much cash will be available, put it all into one wedding account. This will make keeping track of what is being spent much simpler than if the money were mixed up with everyday expenses.

To get a clear picture of how the budget needs to be split, use the formula outlined in the next column. It will work with any budget, and, once you can put a real amount next to each element, you will quickly see whether your proposed venue is affordable or whether you need to think again.

reception, including food and drink	40%
venue/ceremony/musicians	15%
outfits	10%
flowers/entertainment/transport	10%
photography/video	7%
stationery	3%
honeymoon	10%
unexpected extras	5%
total budget	**100%**

This formula is based on averages, so it's fine if you want to spend more in one area than what's given here, but remember that you'll have to compromise somewhere else in order to balance the totals.

OPPOSITE Wherever possible, make use of outdoor spaces, arranging tables and chairs and using lighting to create a party atmosphere in the open air.

BELOW For a modern reception, and if weather allows, hold the party outside in the sunshine. At this venue, white umbrellas are used to shade the tables, and the relaxed theme is enhanced by wooden chairs and sky-blue menus and place cards.

CREATIVE COST-CUTTING

If the total budget is looking a little lean and unlikely to finance the beautiful wedding you had imagined, you will need to do some creative cost-cutting. The secret is to make savings where they are unlikely to be noticed – and, yes, it is possible.

a shorter day The longer your guests are with you, the more you have to spend on looking after them, so shorten the wedding day. Ask for a late-afternoon ceremony slot so there is less time to fill before the sit-down reception.

a weekday wedding Avoid getting married at a weekend. Venues and suppliers are much more likely to offer you a good deal if you marry during the week. A Friday wedding will be viewed by many guests as a lovely start to the weekend.

buffet v. formal sit-down Seating all your guests at tables and serving each course is the most expensive option because of the number of waiting staff needed, so a buffet can make financial sense. Just make sure it suits your style of event. A buffet is unlikely to be the best option if you have a high proportion of older and younger guests who will find queuing and carrying plates difficult.

A-list cocktails Impress your guests by inviting them to a stylish cocktail party with lots of finger food and interesting drinks. A shorter, stylish event will delight most guests. Simply make it clear on the invitation what you are planning and that the wedding will be ending at a set time.

less is more Decorating the ceremony and reception venues can be very costly, especially if you want an abundance of flowers. Ask your florist about using foliage, which is cheaper than flowers, and perhaps creating one or two eye-catching arrangements that, strategically placed, will impress your guests and avoid the need for individual arrangements on every table. You can also save money by having any large arrangements moved from the ceremony to the reception venue while photographs are being taken.

BELOW The beauty of an understated venue is that you can add any kind of style. Here, a country-themed reception is given some lovely rustic touches in the form of a gingham table runner tied with ribbon for the buffet and ceramic jugs to hold wildflower arrangements.

ABOVE RIGHT For a high-summer wedding, using a marquee that can be opened at the sides allows guests to feel that they are dining outside. As evening draws in, this marquee is illuminated by a row of lights running around the top, as well as by decorative lanterns.

OPPOSITE A spectacular see-through marquee is decorated with strings of tiny white lights. A lovely idea for an evening garden party, the arrangement includes a seating area and an outside bar for guests to enjoy, but it offers protection just in case the weather turns bad.

trade secret

'Evening buffet dinners are often left uneaten. Instead, serve evening canapés (such as mini-burgers, mini-fish and chips or bacon butties) or something fun such as a chocolate fountain or ice-cream bar. Also, save the cake for the evening, when people are more likely to eat it.'

Charles Howard,
creative director, Jalapeno London

THE WEDDING BUDGETER

You will want to keep track of your budget every step of the way. First, write down an estimate of the amount of money you would ideally like to spend on each part of the wedding. Once you have actually paid for something, put this amount in the actual column, with the difference in the third column. You can then see at a glance whether you are overspending.

category	estimate	actual	difference + or −
ceremony			
licence fee			
location fee			
officiant fee			
music			
wedding outfits			
bride's dress			
headdress			
veil			
accessories			
shoes			
lingerie			
hair			
make-up			
groom's outfit			
accessories			
bridesmaids' dresses			
accessories			
rings			
bride's wedding ring			
groom's wedding ring			

category	estimate	actual	difference + or −
reception			
location fee			
rentals			
(linens, chair backs etc.)			
food			
waiting staff			
wine			
champagne			
soft drinks			
evening bar			
cake			
favours			
flowers/decorations			
ceremony decoration			
bride's bouquet			
bridesmaids' bouquets			
buttonholes			
corsages			
centrepieces			
cake-table flowers			
reception/venue flowers			
flowers for the mothers			
music			
ceremony musicians			
reception musicians			
evening band/DJ			

category	estimate	actual	difference + or −
photography/video			
photographer's fee			
videographer's fee			
prints/video			
disposable cameras			
stationery			
save-the-date cards			
invitations/RSVP cards			
stamps			
order of service			
seating plan			
place cards			
menus			
thank-you cards			
transport			
bride's car			
maids' and mothers' car			
groom's self-drive car			
shuttle bus			
parking fees			
miscellaneous			
wedding organizer			
wedding insurance			
attendants' gifts			
tips			

Allow 5–10 per cent of the total budget for unexpected expenses.

CEREMONY CONSIDERATIONS

There is plenty of published information available on wording and hymn suggestions for the marriage service, but with regard to ceremony style here are a few ideas to make your 'I do' moment even more magical.

straight from the heart

The order of service for a religious ceremony is rather rigid and there are few opportunities to make major changes to the wording, but you can nevertheless include meaningful moments by choosing hymns and readings that have a special significance to you as a couple.

A civil ceremony allows you much more flexibility, including the chance to write your own marriage vows – or at least part of them – if you want to. If you are looking for inspiration, make a list of words that are most appropriate to the way you feel about each other, your relationship and your future together. Is there a line or two from a favourite song or poem that you could 'borrow' to include in your vows? Don't feel you have to write anything lengthy. A few carefully chosen lines on how you feel about your partner and the commitment you are making will be more than enough to bring a tear to the eye to everyone present.

A civil ceremony also gives you the opportunity to move away from the traditional musical accompaniment and include a variety of popular music as you make your entrance, during the signing of the register and as you leave the ceremony as husband and wife.

meaningful moments – ideas for special touches that will help to make your ceremony memorable

* light unity candles to symbolize the joining together of two families
* sprinkle the aisle with fresh petals or lavender heads that will release a wonderful fragrance as the bride makes her entrance
* present each guest with a pack of wedding tissues together with the order of service
* forget the formality of seating the bride's family on the left and the groom's on the right, and ask friends and family to mingle
* give each guest a miniature bottle of bubbles to blow instead of throwing confetti
* release a pair of doves as you leave the ceremony as husband and wife

inspirational phrases

✳ all that I am, I give to you; all that I have,
I share with you

✳ for as long as we both shall live

✳ from this day forward

✳ I will always be by your side

✳ my partner in life, whatever it may bring

✳ this is my solemn vow to you

✳ you are my one true love, above all others

sample wedding vows – to get you started

'I, ..., choose you, ..., as my soul mate and lifelong companion.'
'Together, we will be stronger than we could ever be alone.'
'Through the good and the bad, I want you always by my side.'

'When you need someone to encourage you, I want it to be me.
When you need a helping hand, I want it to be mine. When you
long for someone to smile at, turn to me. When you have
something to share, share it with me.'

'In sickness, I will nurse you back to health. In health, I will
encourage you on your chosen road. In sadness, I will help you to
remember the good times. In happiness, I will make precious
memories with you. In poverty, I will do all that I can to make our
love rich. And in wealth, I will never let our love grow poor.'

OPPOSITE If you are planning a wedding in the open air, think about creating an arbour where you can exchange your vows. At this Anglo-Indian wedding, a aisle of fresh rose petals leads to a pretty white tent, scattered with floor cushions, where the ceremony is conducted.

ABOVE LEFT All eyes will be on the altar at a church wedding so consider spending part of your flower budget on dramatic pedestal arrangements to frame the area where you will say your vows. Your florist can arrange to have them moved to the reception after the ceremony.

THE GUEST LIST

Once you have made the crucial decisions about the type of event you want to plan and how much money you can afford to spend, the time has come to think about who you want to invite.

Guest numbers depend to a large extent on three things: the size of the venue, the mood you are trying to create, and what you are able to afford. Paying for the reception will absorb the lion's share of any wedding budget, and the more people you invite, the more it will cost.

It is usual to split the guest numbers equally between the bride and groom, with family coming first, followed by close friends, work colleagues, friends from school, university and social club memberships. If one or other family is particularly large, there may need to be number-juggling early on in order to accommodate everyone.

Most people will expect to be able to bring their partners, although it is not necessary to invite dates for single friends, unless numbers are unlimited. It is polite to invite the vicar, rabbi or celebrant and his or her partner to the reception.

The decision about whether or not to include children on your guest list will depend on your own attitude and the type of event you envisage. Small children can bring much joy to any occasion but they also get bored easily and tend to be noisy. One solution is to establish a temporary crèche, where trained staff will entertain the little ones during the meal and speeches.

If numbers are very tight, you may want to make yours an adults-only wedding, in which case you need to make this clear at the start, discreetly asking family and friends to let it be known that children are not invited. If you take this route, make sure you don't relent and let one or two couples bring their offspring, or you will risk upsetting other parents when they realize that some people have been given preferential treatment!

Another way to stretch your budget is to host just close family and friends at a lunch straight after the ceremony and invite the majority of your guests to an evening party only. You will still be expected to serve some food – a simple buffet will suffice – but this is much cheaper than inviting everyone to a formal sit-down meal.

You can expect approximately 10 per cent of your guests to decline, so have a B list ready or simply use the money you've saved to put towards upgrading elsewhere.

OPPOSITE For that essential 'ahh' factor, involve small children in your marriage ceremony as flower girls and ring bearers.

BELOW If you allocate a large part of your budget to excellent food and wine, you are bound to keep your guests smiling. It is always better to provide simple, high-quality fare rather than an elaborate but inferior menu.

location, location

Country house, historic building, contemporary hotel or your own back garden – the choice of wedding venue is almost endless, while the decision you make will set the style and tone for the whole celebration. When doing your research, keep your ideal firmly in mind, and don't compromise until you find that one special place, because so-so simply won't do for your wedding day.

location, location

Your choice of place at which to exchange vows and entertain your guests speaks volumes about your personal wedding style. And selecting the perfect location for your big day will be one of your first, and most important, decisions. The venue sets the scene for the whole event, encapsulating a mood and telling a story to your guests about the day you want them to remember. Locations can be as varied as a church, a synagogue, a historical building, a country hotel, a contemporary loft, a windswept beach or your own back garden.

As you start to plan your ideal day, you will no doubt have some idea of what your dream wedding should look like, and this will guide you towards the style of venue that will complement your vision.

You may already have a venue in mind that satisfies all the criteria. Indeed, many couples plan their wedding around the availability of a particular venue because it has special memories or perhaps because it is just right for their chosen theme. Popular locations can get booked up a very long time in advance, so you may have to be patient if there's only one place that's perfect for you.

Simplify your search by using the internet to get a better idea of what is available in your area. Most couples get married close to where they or their families live, although you may prefer to have a weekend wedding away from home, which involves hiring a venue from Friday to Sunday and asking your guests to stay with you for an extended celebration; in such a case, it doesn't matter a great deal where the venue is, since everyone will be travelling there. In some cases, couples choose a different country altogether, turning the wedding into a mini-holiday for their friends and family.

Venue websites are invaluable for discovering what the venue looks like, both inside and out, and for answering many basic questions about room size, gardens, catering facilities and availability. You should get an idea of whether somewhere looks likely to make your shortlist before bothering to make an appointment to view. One word of caution: if a website looks tired and dated, then it is unlikely that the venue's attitude towards your wedding will be much more inspiring, so it is probably advisable to keep looking.

RIGHT Consider choosing an attention-grabbing ceremony location such as this cathedral.

FAR RIGHT An open-air event is dramatic for totally different reasons – lovely in its simplicity, with just the sky for a backdrop.

OPPOSITE Chic cream linens and chair covers and small centrepieces add gentle touches to a venue steeped in history. One imposing floral arrangement is used to great effect at the bottom of the staircase.

The type of ceremony you are planning will dictate whether or not you need to look for two venues or will be able to hold the ceremony and reception in one place. If you are having a religious ceremony then you are most likely to be using the place of worship in your home town. It is possible to marry outside your area and to find out more details you should speak directly to the priest or celebrant in the venue you would like to use.

Common sense dictates that you should look for a reception venue that's within 30 minutes' drive of the ceremony. If you choose somewhere that involves a long drive, you risk creating a very fragmented day not to mention the chance of losing some of your guests en route! In an ideal world your reception should begin within one hour of the ceremony finishing.

trade secret

'Always work with what you've got and look at ways to enhance what is already there. If there is something you don't like (such as the carpet) don't try too hard to overstyle to cover it up, the danger is you will simply draw attention to it. If it is something you can change by hiring in something else (such as the crockery or linens) then do that.'

Sarah Haywood, wedding coordinator

ABOVE The very simplicity of this minimalist church is what makes it stunning. Guests sit on whitewashed benches, At the altar, tall glass vases holding arum lilies are framed by a white backcloth to which the stylist has artfully attached an abundance of white daisies.

RIGHT Try to reflect a room's features when setting out the furniture. In this case, chairs have been put in a circle to echo the lines of the circular space.

OPPOSITE Outdoor seating gives fine views of the parkland surrounding this historic venue.

possible locations

Plenty of different places can be used to hold a stylish wedding so there is no need to settle for the obvious choices.

* historic hotel
* banqueting hall
* contemporary hotel
* country club
* restaurant or public house
* beach or vineyard
* museum, gallery, photographer's loft
* a boat or yacht
* church function room
* community centre
* school or university
* a garden belonging to you or your family

ceremony considerations

In the UK, a religious ceremony must take place in a church, synagogue or chapel. In many other countries, including the USA, the person conducting the ceremony can travel to a location of your choice. Fees to hire religious buildings vary hugely but usually cover the cost of paying the celebrant, heating and lighting, and minimal decoration with perhaps one or two flower arrangements.

WHAT MAKES THE PERFECT VENUE?

Before you fall in love with a fabulous venue, you need to find out how much it will cost and decide whether you can afford it. Hiring a venue on a Saturday or a Sunday is likely to be more expensive than hiring it on a week day – and the longer you want to stay, the more expensive it will be.

Most venues offer a package that includes the hire of specific rooms for a specified length of time. Larger venues are likely to take bookings for more than one event on the same day, so make sure you find out with who or with what event you could be sharing your day. Also, make sure you ask about the use of any outdoor spaces and check if this will involve extra cost. If the venue is small, you are more likely to hire the whole building for your exclusive use.

If you want to hold the ceremony at the same place as the reception, you will normally have to make independent arrangements with the celebrant rather than expecting the venue to do this for you. This includes making sure that the celebrant is available on your preferred wedding date. It is not unknown for a couple happily to book and confirm their wedding location only to discover that there was no celebrant available on that date to marry them – an expensive mistake!

When you have found a venue that interests you, make an appointment for a viewing and go along armed with a list of questions. Take a digital camera and photograph the entrance, the rooms you may be using, the terraces and gardens. Don't rely on memory because it's easy to forget small but important details such as wall coverings and the position of windows and doors.

ABOVE AND BELOW If you want to stamp your own style on the day, a marquee is a good option. It allows you to start with a blank canvas to which you can add all the colours and details that you love.

BELOW LEFT AND OPPOSITE Among the many advantages of a venue steeped in history is the fact that you don't have to worry about the business of decoration – it's already done for you.

As you look around and compare possible venues, pay particular attention to the ambience. How friendly are the staff? Does the atmosphere feel welcoming and homely or grand and formal? Can you imagine your friends and family feeling relaxed and having a good time in this space?

You should expect to be shown the actual rooms that are available for hire. At many venues these are likely to be empty of all but the most basic furniture and it can be quite a challenge to imagine how they will look when filled with tables. Ask to see pictures from previous weddings to get a clearer picture. Make a note of whether other couples used round tables or long tables or a

OPPOSITE Choose your venue to suit the style of your wedding. If you are planning a cocktail party, look for somewhere with an interesting setting such as this stunning tree-lined atrium.

BELOW A Caribbean ceremony makes allusions to the tropical surroundings in its use of bold colours for table linens and oversized Chinese lanterns.

combination of both. How many guests could be accommodated comfortably in the room? Venues are often happy to cram in lots of tables, but the lack of space may not be what you are looking for to create a relaxed event.

If the specified room is enormous, think about whether number of guests you plan to invite will be enough to create a party atmosphere. You don't want to end up with an empty space and the sense that half your guests didn't turn up. Clever use of partitioning can be the solution.

Make a note of any adjoining rooms or a terrace that can be used for a drinks reception and find out about the proximity of the toilets. It's annoying to have to trek along miles of corridors and up and down stairs every time you need the bathroom!

At this initial meeting, it is important for you to meet the people who will be dealing with your wedding. The venue manager, catering manager and any on-site wedding coordinator will be part of your wedding team, and you need to know that they share your vision – and that you actually like them. If they seem distracted, bored or plain disorganized, warning bells should ring. Whatever the size of your budget, you are entitled to expect excellent service, so, if you are in doubt that these people can deliver on the day, look elsewhere.

questions to ask venue staff

* what is the location hire fee?
* how long is the hire period?
* which rooms can I hire?
* is there an on-site wedding coordinator?
* if not, who will be responsible for my wedding?
* does the venue have on-site catering?
* can I bring in my own catering?
* what is the package per head price?
* are tables, chairs, linens and tableware included?
* can we bring our own alcohol?
* is there a corkage charge?
* will there be other events on the same day?
* is there overnight accommodation?
* are room discounts available for guests?
* can we use the gardens?
* is there room for a marquee?
* is there adequate parking for the number of guests?
* where are the toilets located?
* will the reception have to end at a specified time?
* are there any noise restrictions?
* is the venue child-friendly?
* do we have to pay a deposit?
* when is the balance due?
* what is the cancellation policy?

RIGHT With gardens as beautiful as these, an open-sided marquee is a must, allowing guests to enjoy the view. Here, the addition of flower balls and ribbons in the trees continues the wedding theme into the garden.

FAR RIGHT First impressions count, so make the venue entrance interesting. Potted trees always look stylish, and in this case the floral decorations extend over the door as well.

say yes if the venue has ...

☐ a great location

☐ attentive, knowledgeable staff

☐ a wow! factor (relating to its décor, history or gardens, etc.)

☐ freshly decorated rooms

☐ a modern kitchen

☐ child-friendly areas (if required)

☐ good parking facilities

say no if the venue has ...

☐ uninspiring or uninterested staff

☐ so-so décor

☐ areas in need of a coat of paint

☐ no kitchen

☐ no outside space

☐ poor parking or is difficult for guests to find

WILL IT WORK FOR YOU?

Every style of venue has good and bad points that need to be carefully weighed up before you agree to sign on the dotted line.

historical venue

Nothing will make you feel more special than getting married in a fairytale castle or an opulent mansion filled with antiques. On the other hand, a historical venue is likely to be the most expensive style of building to hire and there may be restrictions on guests regarding access and use of furnishings.

city hotel

The ballroom of a large city hotel is a popular choice for weddings, and guests will love the easy accessibility. Hotels are likely to be experienced at holding wedding celebrations and the service should be first-rate. Style options are limited, so, if you are looking for a place on which you can stamp your personality, a hotel is probably not for you. Outdoor space may be limited or non-existent.

country hotel

For couples who are attracted by the organized environment of a hotel but would also like some great outside space, a country hotel with large gardens is an obvious choice. Interior decoration may be dated, so make sure the allure of the outdoors doesn't blind you to any shortcomings inside. The weather may let you down, leaving you with a so-so reception in a boring function room.

contemporary space

An empty space that can be transformed by your vision is a lovely idea, and a good solution for anyone who doesn't fancy the traditional wedding trimmings. However, such an arrangement involves a lot of work since everything from food to tables and chairs needs to be brought to the venue. The services of a wedding organizer may be required.

themed venue

Choosing a venue with a quirky or unusual theme is the quick route to a distinctively personal day. Plenty of different venues are available for hire, from sports grounds to zoos, from museums to ships, from wineries to fairgrounds. But don't forget you are planning a wedding; there should be some elements to reflect the solemnity and traditions associated with the commitment of marriage.

marquee/tent

A marquee/tent is a great way of expanding a venue you love that's short of space, or of making it possible for you to get married at your family home. As is the case with a contemporary space, you will need to bring all the services into the marquee/ tent, which can be time-consuming to arrange.

beach or gardens

Celebrating outside in the sunshine and then enjoying the balmy delights of a summer's evening is a wonderful idea in theory, but no wedding spot is guaranteed perfect weather, so you will need to have a Plan B up your sleeve and provide somewhere to transfer the party in case of rain.

trade secret

'Think about your guest list first – the number of people you want to invite will help you to narrow down your choice of venue. And be sure to check whether the venue can help you to decorate the rooms you'll be using as part of their fee. The backdrop of beautiful gardens or a ready-decorated Christmas hall can provide you with a stylish event for less.'

Colette Harris, editor
You & Your Wedding magazine

TOP LEFT AND RIGHT Historical buildings are ideal for traditional weddings but will 'feel' wrong if the rest of the day is contemporary in character.

ABOVE A beach setting is obviously an informal option and, to suit the outdoor mood, you need to keep all the elements relaxed.

LEFT If you are unable to find the perfect venue, a marquee is an attractive alternative because it allows you to create a room that reflects your dream right down to the smallest details.

ALL IN THE DETAILS

So you think you've found an ideal venue that fulfils all the criteria on your wish list. What next? The first thing to do is to make a provisional booking to secure your preferred date. This doesn't mean that you've actually booked the venue, but it expresses your intention to book, and there is usually a set period of time before final confirmation is required. Some venues will ask for a deposit at this stage; others will be happy with a written request. If you are asked to pay a deposit, check whether or not this is refundable – many venues will keep your cash if you change your mind.

Expect to receive from the venue staff a written quotation covering everything discussed at your initial meeting. Apart from the date and time of your wedding, it should include fees for location hire, catering, drinks, waiting staff, car-parking attendants and whatever else you requested. Check through this document carefully to make sure it represents your wishes and to ascertain that nothing has been added in or left out. Does the total include all taxes and service charges? In the UK, VAT at 17.5 per cent adds considerably to the final cost. If no service charge is mentioned, reckon on paying an extra 15 per cent in gratuities.

Depending on the venue, either you will be booking a wedding package, which includes hire of location, tables and linens, food, drinks and waiting staff, or every cost will be itemized separately. The package is usually priced per head, so it is easy to work out the total cost once you are certain of guest numbers. Within this package there are likely to be several menu options at varying prices reflecting the choice of food. Wines are usually priced separately, ranging from a relatively cheap house option to very expensive fine wines. If you are thinking about providing your own wines, make

sure you check whether there is a corkage charge. This is an amount added by the venue to cover the cost of chilling, opening and serving the wine to your guests. It is usually charged per bottle and can be rather high, with the result that what might have seemed like an economical expenditure on wine is no longer the most cost-effective option.

You are likely to receive an itemized estimate if you want to deviate from the classic items offered by most venues – for example, if you want to use coloured glasses and coloured linens that need to be sourced from elsewhere, or if you want to put up a marquee/tent or bring in your own caterers. If you are using several suppliers, bringing them all together to an event space that doesn't have extensive on-site facilities, you will need to obtain estimates from each supplier as well as from the venue itself, all of which need to be checked to make sure nothing has been forgotten. Read the small print for details of how and when all monies are due. Never pay everything in advance; expect

BELOW If the view from a window is less than lovely, add a row of tall, slim vases and a line-up of votives to give guests something pretty to look at.

to retain a percentage that will be payable on the day or within seven days of the event. Find out whether the hours you have booked include time for set up or if this is extra? What are the charges for overtime? What equipment is there on site for entertainment (sound system, dance floor, etc.)? Are there any rules about the type of music you can play and when it has to stop? Are there any restrictions on where you can take photographs?

Can you use candles? If the venue contains many valuable antiques, there may be a ban on naked flame, which will certainly curtail any romantic notions you may have about dining by candlelight.

Be aware of the insurance position. Does the venue have adequate cover in case someone is injured or damages some of the fixtures and fittings? Do you need to take out extra liability insurance of your own to cover every eventuality?

ABOVE An all-white wedding always looks wonderful because it is so simple. At this venue, the couple have added a clever mirrored dance floor that is spotlit as night falls.

perfect palettes

Beautiful weddings are all about colour. Whether you choose pastels or vibrant brights, calming neutrals or classic whites, you are aiming for a symphony of tones that is easy on the eye yet impressive enough to live in everyone's memory long after the last swirls of confetti have been swept away.

perfect palettes

Every stylish wedding draws on a distinctive colour palette at various important moments during the day. It is up to you to decide whether this is a riot of brights or something simple and traditional such as white on white. Establishing a colour theme is the best way to make sure that everything looks well coordinated and is appropriate to the type of wedding, the venue and the time of year.

A good starting point for choosing a theme is to think about your favourite colours. In the first chapter you will have learned about creating a mood board in order to get a better understanding of the overall vision for the day, and choosing your colour palette can be done in much the same way. All of us have colours we are naturally drawn to, a particular shade or intensity that we prefer over something else. Make a colour inspiration board of images torn from magazines and look at paint colour charts for subtle tonal variations to find the exact match that's lurking in your imagination. Look at the predominant colours in your wardrobe and those used to decorate your home, and a portfolio of the colours you like to have around you will begin to emerge.

The style and décor of your location is also something that should be considered before any colour choices are finalized, so it is advisable not to order anything until after the venue has been booked. This is particularly true in older-style buildings, where the carpets and curtains may be strongly patterned and could clash horribly with your favoured shades. If in doubt, the safest choice is often to opt for a predominantly white wedding, because white works in just about any location, looking cool in summer but appropriately clean and crisp at a winter wedding. You can then introduce a few touches of a highlighter colour to avoid an overall effect that is excessively stark.

LEFT Colour-coordinated baskets, tied with ribbon, are filled with fresh or freeze-dried petals for flower girls to scatter as they walk up the aisle.

OPPOSITE A vibrant palette of orange and lime green is just what is needed to offset the stark white interior of a marquee/tent. The open sides of the marquee have been lined with orange sheers that can be lifted to let in sunshine or closed when night falls.

the colour mood board

Creating a mood board that incorporates your favourite colours is always a good place to start when devising a colour palette.

what works with white?

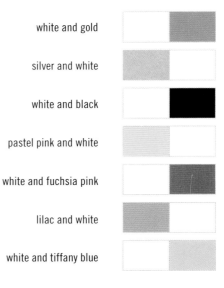

white and gold

silver and white

white and black

pastel pink and white

white and fuchsia pink

lilac and white

white and tiffany blue

trade secret

'The colour theme for your wedding needs to be individual and unique. Don't always base a theme on your favourite colour; it should ultimately depend on the season and overall style of your wedding. Nor does the colour of the bridesmaids' dresses have to dictate the entire colour scheme of your wedding. Remember two things: be imaginative and less is more.'

Anthony Del Col, wedding stylist

perfect colour combinations

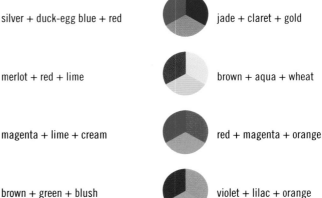

silver + duck-egg blue + red

jade + claret + gold

merlot + red + lime

brown + aqua + wheat

magenta + lime + cream

red + magenta + orange

brown + green + blush

violet + lilac + orange

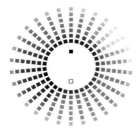

THE COLOUR WHEEL

For help in deciding which colours to include in your palette, use a traditional colour wheel. Red, orange, yellow, green, blue, indigo and violet – according to established colour theory, adjacent colours harmonize well but, if you are seeking to make a flamboyant statement, opposites combine to more dramatic effect. The wheel will help you establish the basics, after which you can think about the possible variations within your chosen colours, since every one will have many tones. What you don't want to do is to fixate on one tone and try to make everything match it exactly. An all-white wedding can be visually stunning, but too much of any other single colour is a step too far.

Choose your favourite palette and then use subtle variations to bring a sense of harmony to everything from the invitations to the table settings. If you want contrasting colours, look at those on the opposite sides of the wheel from each other, but remember to choose combinations that are in keeping with the season. Red and green look great together but create an instant association with winter festivities, which would be strange if you were having a spring wedding. Pastels are better suited to a wedding in warm weather, when rooms are likely to be full of light.

Colours should also be in keeping with the style of wedding. Fresh, light colours such as blue, white, yellow and pink suit a beach wedding. A Valentine's Day theme would naturally focus on red, and a September wedding will feel right dressed in a palette of russet, orange, gold and greens.

LEFT A very simple touch such as tying a theme-appropriate coloured ribbon around a vase is all that's needed to give tables and flowers a coordinated look.

ABOVE For a seasonal splash of vibrant colour, think about arrangements that use just one species of flower such as these amazing yellow calla lilies.

trade secret

what's your style?

Most of us fall into one of three categories when it comes to the colours we like.

primary palette
black and white, red and white, silver/gold and white, white on white

princess palette
pastel pink, blue, lilac, green, chocolate – all paired with ivory or white

modern palette
black, brown, fuchsia, lime, purple, orange, aqua – mixed with each other

OPPOSITE A simple palette of yellow and white is anything but boring when you have spectacular table arrangements. This towering vase is filled with colourless gel rather than water and topped with an oversize spray of brilliant yellow orchids.

RIGHT You can never go wrong with the classic colour combinations such as pink and white, yellow and white, and lilac and white. This centrepiece is an irresistible mix of cream and yellow roses interspersed with white stocks.

BRIGHT AND BEAUTIFUL

There was a time when every bride had a white wedding, with just the merest hint of another colour to accent the reception party. These days, as nuptials become less traditional and brides more adventurous, you are more likely to see a palette of anything up to five different colours at a wedding celebration – for example, an English country garden theme might include pink, lemon, green, lilac and brown to echo the beauty of a warm summer's afternoon.

When it comes to the effective use of single or multiple colours, the trick is to incorporate them subtly throughout the day for a wedding that has a well-coordinated feel but doesn't look like you've tried too hard. Over-emphasis on colour matching is never a successful strategy. You want to use elements from your palette on the stationery, at the ceremony, the cocktail party and at the reception. The touches can be small – even a mere flash of a certain colour is enough to convince the eye that you have created a beautiful theme.

Colour is said to have a powerful effect on mood, which is worth bearing in mind when making colour choices for your wedding.

red	raises the energy in a room and helps to create excitement (and irritability)
pink	all shades of pink have a calming effect; a strong pink is said to act as an appetite suppressant
yellow	communicates happiness and the warmth of sunshine
blue	calming, relaxing and even said to lower blood pressure
green	restful and calming and ideal to combine with yellow and blue
purple	rich, elegant, sophisticated; associated with luxury
orange	an energetic colour, creating excitement and fun
brown	muted and relaxing with strong connections to chocolate
black	powerful and best kept as an accent colour; depressing in large quantities
white	fresh and clean, but can be stark and 'chilly' if it is not combined with other colours

LEFT If you think hired chairs will look too plain, you can also hire coloured seat pads and mark the end of each row with a posy of colour-coordinated flowers.

FAR LEFT Fabric strips in the shape of Chinese happiness symbols are dotted with fresh orchids and used to decorate the chairs of the bride and groom.

OPPOSITE For a winter wedding, choose bouquets and bridesmaids' posies in a rich red to contrast elegantly with the creamy white of the dresses.

LEFT Even the ribbon with which you choose to tie the order of service at the ceremony should coordinate with the rest of the wedding palette.

INVITATIONS

The first opportunity you have to tell the world about your chosen colour palette is in the design of the invitations, so make the most of it. You could use coloured card and envelopes or have a white card and use colours from your palette as accent features by incorporating, for example, a coloured monogram or a coloured ribbon.

CEREMONY LOCATION

If you are planning to hold a religious ceremony in one location and the reception in another, you could have two entirely different colour themes, each in keeping with the décor of the venue. In fact, it will probably be more successful to take this approach since it is unlikely that both locations will suit your theme perfectly. Church interiors tend to be fairly dark, so, if you are getting married in church, choose either predominantly white or brightly coloured flowers for any arrangements.

OUTFITS

There is nothing to say that the bride has to be dressed all in white. Look at subtle variations on the theme such as ivory, cream and gold, or throw tradition to the wind and wear a pink, yellow or red dress. Accent a white gown with a coloured sash, wear coloured shoes or a veil trimmed with colour and tie your bouquet with coordinating ribbon.

Your groom and his best man can get involved in the colour theme by wearing a coordinating tie, waistcoat or cummerbund and a buttonhole (but not all at once – one or two touches of colour with a dark suit will suffice).

It is in the design of the bridesmaids' dresses that the colour theme of a wedding is traditionally

trade secret

'While pure white can flatter a rosy complexion, warmer tones look best on a darker skin. In winter, when natural light tends to be grey, ivories and off-whites enhance women and lend an air of subtle sophistication to the gown.'

Vera Wang, wedding dress designer

brought to the fore. The bridesmaids can either all wear identical dresses or, for a more modern look, they can wear coordinated separates in various tones of the same colour. This allows each girl to wear something that suits her shape and her personal taste. Flower girls look cutest in party dresses; you can reflect your colour theme in waist sashes and ribbons for their hair.

FLOWERS

Flowers are available in just about every shade that can be imagined, so you should be able to create a bouquet and centrepieces that incorporate the key elements of your palette. If your favourite colour is out of season, use white flowers and reflect the theme in your choice of containers or plain vases decorated with wide coloured ribbons.

BELOW A popular choice for weddings, lilac looks pretty all year round. These bridesmaids' dresses are tied with sashes in a pale lilac that perfectly matches the ribbon ties on the posies of summer roses.

THE WEDDING CAKE

When considering how to use your colour palette, you may be attracted to the idea of creating a colour-coordinated cake; this can be successful as long is it is done extremely well. Specialist cake makers should have the expertise to match any colour you choose to perfection. Just remember that brightly coloured food is rarely appealing and steer clear of anything too garish if you want to tempt the taste buds.

A safer alternative is to have a predominantly white cake and decorate this with flowers and ribbons to suit your theme.

trade secret

'I always ask my clients to approach their wedding with an open mind and this includes decisions about the colour palette. A couple with contemporary personal style can easily fall in love with an English castle as the place to host their wedding celebrations. The location frequently dictates the colour scheme. A Spanish-style venue may lend itself to deep reds, while an art gallery might call for bold arrangements in crisp whites. I also try to incorporate the feel of the celebration. Is it to be a black-tie formal affair or is there a Balinese twist that calls for brightly coloured silk in the décor?'

Jo Gartin,
author and wedding coordinator

ABOVE Fresh flowers are a stylish option for decorating a simple cake. Here the bride has chosen purple hydrangeas for her white chocolate cake.

LEFT Matching linens and seat cushions are saved from looking over-coordinated by the gold chairs and splashes of white from the candles and flowers.

TABLES FOR ALL SEASONS

The reception tables will look most spectacular when dressed in colours that are linked with the time of year at which your wedding takes place.

spring tables

colour palette: pretty pastels – pink, green, yellow, blue, lavender
Spring is the season for all things fresh and fun. Make sure your tables reflect this by bringing the spring sunshine into your reception.

* Give each table a vintage English tea-party theme using patterned tablecloths and floral teacups and saucers in a combination of pinks, greens and yellows. Frame black and white photographs of members of the bride's and groom's families and put these on mantelpieces and on the escort-card table.

* For a contemporary twist, use fresh gingham linens, colour-coordinated plates and coloured glassware.

* Fill wooden baskets or enamel buckets with a profusion of pink, green, lavender and yellow flowers and place these on the tables as a substitute for traditional centrepieces.

summer tables

colour palette: country garden or bright and zesty
Summer weddings tend to go one of two ways, celebrating the overblown richness of the season with either a classic country garden feel or a hot, tropical theme incorporating lots of bright colour.

* Tables should look clean and simple with lots of crisp white linens. Cutlery/flatware and glassware needs to sparkle.

* Line clear glass vases with leaves and fill with old-fashioned summer roses or peonies in full bloom. Alternatively, line the table with tiny potted plants that can double as favours.

* Shade guests from the heat of the sun with oversize white umbrellas, or dine in the shade of a patio trellis under a 'ceiling' covered with colourful Chinese paper lanterns.

RIGHT A light-flooded venue such as this conservatory allows you to make a success of just about any colour combination. Soft green satin linens, silver chairs, cream napkins and silver chargers combine to create a sense of relaxed tranquillity.

autumn/fall tables

colour palette: orange, russet, yellow, gold, copper, purple
Autumn has a harvest feel and the obvious approach is to echo the colours of nature at this time of year.

* Think rustic elegance with crisp leaves rimming table centrepieces; speak to your florist about using berries to highlight your bouquet and to display in large vases as statement arrangements.
* The glorious orange of pumpkins make them ideal as decorations and as part of the menu. Serve pumpkin soup from hollowed-out pumpkin shells and pile miniature pumpkins as table arrangements.
* Make the most of the countryside theme by using rustic buckets to hold arrangements and put vintage candelabra on each table. Create place cards by writing the names of each guest on a tag attached to a gold skeleton leaf.

winter tables

colour palette: winter white or the rich hues of the festive season
A winter table should be warm and inviting, brimming with candlelight, sumptuous jewel colours or icy sparkle.

* Use gold or red chargers at each place setting. Hire gilt-decorated goblets instead of traditional wine glasses.
* On rectangular tables, use a shimmering chiffon table runner that will sparkle by candlelight. Hire chair covers in jewel colours or white chair covers tied with coloured ribbons. Or you could hire a velvet cushion for each chair in a colour that reflects your décor.
* Buy large quantities of cheap Christmas baubles and heap them into tall glass vases to make centrepieces. Use more ornate decorations at each place setting that double as a name tag and a favour.

ABOVE LEFT Why search outside the season for colour inspirations when it's Halloween? This couple served soup from hollowed-out pumpkins.

LEFT There's nothing to say that you need to use more than one colour. Here, roses and orchids, both in vibrant orange, create an elegant table.

OPPOSITE A wedding in the winter festive season means you can have fun with colour – and, in this case at least, there's no hint of red. A gold-and-white theme always looks stylish, and the addition of bells, crackers and miniature gold fir cones is bound to amuse your guests.

so inviting

Formal, thematic or whimsical, your choice of wedding stationery says a lot about the style of your forthcoming nuptials. Invitations offer a tantalizing glimpse into the type of event your guests will be attending. Beautifully coordinated paper items – from the order of service to the cards on a towering wishing tree – go a long way towards creating a memorable occasion.

so inviting

Wedding stationery provides your guests with the first indication of what is to come, offering them essential guidance about the style of the event they will be attending. Invitations also indicate the level of formality to be expected, so it's important that you choose a form of invitation that reflects how you envisage the look and feel of the day.

Invitations can reveal a lot about the bride's and groom's aspirations for the wedding. It is not only the words you write on the page that convey a message; it's the design of the stationery itself. And invitations are just the first part of what should be a well-coordinated series of printed items. At the same time as designing invitations, you should consider the order of service, the seating plan, the menus, table numbers and thank-you cards.

Start by thinking about what message you want to send to guests about your wedding. A traditional white card or simple folded invitation

suits a formal wedding, but for a more informal occasion you can let your imagination run riot and design an individual invitation, personalized around you and your groom. Continuity is the key if you want to create a lasting impression, and the use of a monogram or an icon such as a heart or favourite flower is a stylish design feature that can be used to tie all your stationery together.

The many different stationery sources include stationery companies, wedding specialists, high-street department stores and the internet. You can buy cheap pre-printed cards to fill in yourself or have a bespoke package, tailor-made to the last detail. It all depends on you and your budget.

BELOW If in doubt, choose a classic card. You don't have to go for white or cream; this chocolate-brown card with silver writing looks very impressive.

BOTTOM Bespoke stationery can be designed to match your colour scheme perfectly. This couple chose cards in two shades of lilac with a pretty laser-cut butterfly pattern.

trade secret

'Invitations should capture each couple's personal fairy tale, so make sure your stationer knows as much detail as possible about the wedding in order to create something personal just for you.'

Susan O'Hanlon, bespoke stationer

INVITATION STYLE

You should aim to choose invitations that reflect the type of wedding you are planning.

formal or informal

A wedding involving a religious ceremony and black-tie reception demands a traditional invitation, whereas a more relaxed hand-decorated invitation would be perfectly suitable for a contemporary civil wedding. Your guests will take their cue from your invitations on how much to dress up.

the theme

If you have chosen a colour theme for the wedding, incorporate this in your invitations. If butterflies or hearts are a big part of your day, make them a big part of the invitations too.

TOP Invitations offer the first clues to the style and colour theme of the day, so make sure they send the right messages.

LEFT When ordering invitations, speak to your stationer about coordinating other paper items such as place cards and menus.

ABOVE Invitations need to tell guests about the when, where and how of the forthcoming wedding, but you could also add a few lines from a favourite poem and then stamp your personality on the card with a seal bearing the entwined initials of you and your partner.

personal taste

If you are known as a fun-loving couple, then your guests may think a traditional invitation isn't exactly your style. Everything about your wedding should be an accurate reflection of the two of you.

big or small

If you are having a small wedding, you can indulge in personalized invitations, perhaps something handmade and very individual. If you are having a large wedding, or need to include other information such as directions and hotel information in the same envelope, plain and simple is probably best.

ABOVE RIGHT A simple card coloured brown and pink to reflect the wedding palette has been decorated with roses to match the bride's bouquet.

RIGHT Tying your invitations with pretty ribbon is a lovely finishing touch and adds to the recipients' anticipation as they open their personal envelopes.

BELOW RIGHT The invitation envelope can also contain essential information such as a map showing the location of the venue with helpful hints on nearby parking and websites for local transport. Many stationers can print these to complement the style of your stationery.

trade secret

'Wedding stationery is designed to be a reflection of the couple's personal style as well as giving a glimpse into the style of the wedding day. I always advise couples to choose the calligraphy/illustration style of the invitation first — whether it is a sophisticated affair, an intimate garden ceremony or a funky beach wedding. From there, the colours are chosen as well as the type of paper and printing technique.'

Stephannie Barba,
Couture Calligraphy and Stationery

PRINTING STYLES

The price of invitations varies as much as the style and depends very much on where you buy them.

engraving

Usually used for ultra-formal invitations, engraving is the most expensive form of printing. It involves preparing a metal plate engraved with the wording and then stamping this onto paper from the back, giving a raised appearance on the front.

thermography

A more cost-effective alternative, used by many big stationery companies, thermography produces an effect that looks much like engraving. The only real way to tell the difference is that the back of the letters produced by thermography will feel smooth; engraved lettering has been pushed into the paper.

embossing

Another expensive technique, embossing creates individual letters that are raised and shiny. It is often used for the couple's initials and is perfect if you want your invitations to look extra-special.

offset printing

The most cost-effective method of printing, offset is used for many styles of invitation. It offers the most flexibility for contemporary invitations using different types of paper, incorporating the use of decoration, coloured inks and photographs.

ABOVE The typeface you select for your invitations reveals a great deal about the formality of the occasion. Swirls and monograms are traditional.

LEFT Contemporary oversize lettering tells your guests that the wedding is likely to have an informal feel.

BELOW A couple tying the knot in the South of France chose this retro-style drawing of St Tropez to adorn their invitations.

CALLIGRAPHY

If you would like to handwrite the names of your guests onto your invitations but are aware that your writing is not really good enough for the task, consider employing the services of a professional calligrapher. This age-old art of handwriting is very attractive but expensive because it is so time-consuming. The budget-conscious option is to use a computer package that can reproduce a similar look at a fraction of the price.

LETTERING STYLES

Most stationers will offer you a choice of fonts for the lettering inside your invitation. There are hundreds of different options but here are some of the most popular choices for wedding stationery; each one tells you something about the style of the occasion and whether it is going to be traditional or contemporary.

Charlotte Louise and Robert Parker
Shelly Andante

Charlotte Louise and Robert Parker
Snell Roundhand

Charlotte Louise and Robert Parker
American Typewriter

Charlotte Louise and Robert Parker
Times

Charlotte Louise and Robert Parker
Century Gothic

Charlotte Louise and Robert Parker
Helvetica

CHARLOTTE LOUISE AND ROBERT PARKER
BANK GOTHIC

TRADITIONAL INVITATION WORDING

A wedding invitation normally comes from the individuals who will be hosting the occasion. According to tradition, this is the bride's parents, but today it can just as easily be the groom's parents or the couple themselves. If you are unsure of the correct wording, look at one of the many wedding websites or ask your stationer for advice – and don't be afraid to adapt traditional wording to suit your family circumstances.

bride's parents as wedding hosts

Mr and Mrs John Brown
request the pleasure of your company
at the marriage of their daughter
Charlotte Louise
to
Mr Robert Parker
4.00pm Saturday 16 May 2010
at St Paul's Cathedral, London
and afterwards for dinner and dancing in
The Dorchester Hotel, Park Lane
London
RSVP to Mrs John Brown, [insert telephone number]
by 2 April 2010
(you can request the honour of your guests' company
if the wedding is very formal)

couple as hosts

Ms Charlotte Louise Brown
and
Mr Robert Parker
request the pleasure of your company
at their marriage
4.00pm Saturday 16 May 2010
at St Paul's Cathedral, London
and afterwards for dinner and dancing at
The Dorchester Hotel, Park Lane
London
RSVP to Charlotte Brown, [insert telephone number]
by 2 April 2010

single or widowed parent as host

Mr John Brown
requests the pleasure of your company
at the marriage of his daughter
Charlotte Louise
to
Mr Robert Parker
4.00pm Saturday 16 May 2010
at St Paul's Cathedral, London
and afterwards for dinner and dancing at
The Dorchester Hotel, Park Lane
London
RSVP to John Brown
[insert telephone number]
by 2 April 2010

divorced and remarried parent as hosts

Mr John Brown and Mrs Vanessa Brown
request the pleasure of your company
at the marriage of Mr Brown's daughter
Charlotte Louise
to
Mr Robert Parker
4.00pm Saturday 16 May 2010
at St Paul's Cathedral, London
and afterwards for dinner and dancing at
The Dorchester Hotel, Park Lane
London
RSVP Mrs Vanessa Brown
[insert telephone number]
by 2 April 2010

divorced parents as hosts

Mr John Brown and Mrs Julie Smith
request the pleasure of your company
at the marriage of their daughter
Charlotte Louise
to
Mr Robert Parker
4.00pm Saturday 16 May 2010
at St Paul's Cathedral, London
and afterwards for dinner and dancing at
The Dorchester Hotel, Park Lane
London
RSVP Mrs Julie Smith
[insert telephone number]
by 2 April 2010

It is usual to leave a space within the invitation to write in the guests' names or to write their names in the top right hand corner.

BELOW Graphic images of the initials of the bride and groom form the basis of one of the most successful themes for a wedding. They can be added to everything from the invitations to the cake decorations.

INFORMAL INVITATION WORDING

An invitation with more relaxed wording is probably better suited to a contemporary wedding and is most appropriate when the bride and groom, rather than their parents, are hosts.

example 1

It is with great joy that we invite you
to celebrate our marriage
Charlotte Brown & Robert Parker
2.00 pm on Saturday 16 May 2010
St Mary's Chapel
and afterwards for
Cocktails and dancing under the stars
The Rose Bush Hotel
San Francisco
Dress to impress

example 2

CHARLOTTE BROWN & ROBERT PARKER
TOGETHER WITH THEIR PARENTS
REQUEST THE PLEASURE OF YOUR
COMPANY
AS THEY BECOME HUSBAND AND WIFE
FIVE O'CLOCK ON SATURDAY AFTERNOON
16 MAY 2010
THE RIVER GARDENS, SUNSET DRIVE
WEST HOLLYWOOD
BLACK TIE OPTIONAL

LEFT AND BELOW Bring a personal touch to a smaller wedding with handmade stationery. This style of bespoke paperwork is pricey but can be tailored to suit your colour scheme and include all sorts of personal details from illustrations to a location map and elaborate calligraphy.

trade secret

'Unless your envelopes are self-seal, use a glue stick to seal them. This prevents the unsightly buckling effect you frequently get with the 'lick and stick' method. A blob of sealing wax embossed with your monogram is a stylish way to finish off the envelope.'

Vanessa Gore, wedding stylist

sent with style

Give your guests a flavour of what's to come with a modern themed invitation. Be creative with labels – there are lots of printers who offer a customized service. Attach your customized label to a fortune cookie (Oriental theme), a seashell (beach wedding), a sachet of hot chocolate (winter wedding) or a cocktail umbrella (summer picnic). Small empty boxes that you can use for mailing are available from favour companies. Accent each invitation with a suitable icon such as a pressed flower, a pearl button, a tiny golden heart or a shell. Download your favourite romantic song onto a blank CD and stick a customized invitation label in the centre. Or customize a blank CD sleeve and use this as the invitation. Print the invitation onto coloured paper, roll and tie with decorated twine, then mail in a cardboard tube.

spell check

Stationery is expensive and you don't want to make any costly mistakes on your wedding invitations. When you receive a proof, check and double check the details and the spellings before giving the printer the go-ahead. Make sure you like the layout and that it reflects the style of the rest of the day.

ABOVE Colour co-ordinated envelopes are a nice finishing touch for informal invitations and widely available from specialist stationers and department stores.

BELOW If many of your guests are travelling some distance to join you, try to add as much helpful location information as possible in your invitation, including a map.

DETAILS, DETAILS

Always order more invitations than you think you need – at least 25 extra to allow for mistakes and for inviting 'replacement' guests at the last minute; at a large wedding you should expect about 10 per cent of your 'A-list' guests to be unable to come. Remember to send an invitation to your ceremony officiant; the chances are that he or she won't attend, but it is polite to ask. And keep a couple of pristine invitations for your wedding album.

Envelopes play a part in the overall impression your invitations will make, so think about choosing a style with coloured inserts to match your wedding theme. Most specialist stationers will have a good selection to choose from. You could also use coloured ink to address the envelopes or get some labels printed with a personalized border.

If you are using a mail-order service for your stationery, ask for samples of the exact paper the company will be using and any envelopes before placing the final order. There are so many different papers available, and so many variations in colour, weight and texture, that you will want to be certain you have ordered the right one for you.

Assign the task of monitoring the RSVP list to a trusted relative or friend. This is a job either the mother of the bride or the mother of the groom will probably relish; put her contact details at the bottom of the invitation with an ideal reply date, at least one month before the wedding.

Most of your guests should reply within a fortnight, but some of them may need chasing up. Alternatively, you may like to enclose reply cards and addressed envelopes with the invitations. A printed postcard is the cheapest option.

ABOVE Place cards with names and table numbers are essential so that your guests know where they will be sitting.

LEFT The use of coloured type – here in a vibrant pink to match the napkin – looks fresh and contemporary.

OPPOSITE Save-the-date cards are a good idea, especially if you are getting married in a holiday period when your guests may have other commitments.

trade secret

'Make use of colour, texture and patterns in your additional stationery such as the order of service, the seating plan, tree cards, menus, place cards and thank-you cards to carry your theme and tie your overall concept together.'

Aleit Swanepoel, wedding coordinator

CREATING A WEDDING WEBSITE

Wedding websites are increasingly popular, especially among couples marrying away from home and inviting many guests who will have to travel to an unfamiliar area. Many of the bridal websites let you set up your own personal site for free once you have registered with them. Uploading the information is pretty straightforward and you can even include photographs as plans progress. Some websites allow friends to post messages and photographs as well.

Use your website to post all details and timings, directions to the ceremony and the reception venue (if the reception is being held in a separate building), contact numbers for taxis and local accommodation details. If you are having a wedding weekend, include local restaurant recommendations and even information such as where to find an ATM/cash machine and a pharmacy.

After the wedding you can use the site to post some of your favourite wedding photographs. This will be much appreciated by distant friends and relatives who were unable to join you on the day. If your site allows, it is also a lovely idea to create a 'memories section' and invite guests to post their favourite memories from the day. You can then collect these, print them out and keep them as part of your wedding album.

ADDITIONAL WEDDING STATIONERY

At the same time as looking for invitations, it is worth thinking about the other stationery you may need for your wedding. It is usual, and will give a coordinated look, to use the same design and typestyle for all stationery.

save-the-date cards

These are recommended if you are marrying during the summer months or close to Christmas or Thanksgiving, when many of your guests may be planning vacations or celebrations of their own.

sample save-the-date wording

Charlotte and Robert are getting married
16 May 2010
The River Gardens
West Hollywood
Please save their date

Save-the-date cards can be simple postcards or you can send cards in a variety of other formats – for example, a postcard depicting you and your fiancé as children, printed pencils, a fridge magnet, a packet of flower seeds, a CD or calendar.

invitation reply cards

Reply cards, which can be sent out in the same envelopes as the wedding invitations, are a good idea if you think your guests may be slow to respond to a telephone number or email address printed on the invitation. A 'delete where appropriate' format is usually the best:

Sample reply-card wording

[blank space for the guests' name]
would be delighted to/unfortunately cannot accept
your kind invitation for 16 May 2010

These can either be printed on a postcard or you will need to include a stamped and addressed envelope.

order of service

The order of service is a printed running order of the ceremony. Order-of-service cards are either placed on each chair or handed out by the ushers as guests arrive at the ceremony. The cards detail everything from the arrival of the bride to the recessional, when the couple leave the ceremony as husband and wife.

The format for the order of service should be in keeping with the formality of the wedding. For a religious ceremony, a simple folded card with your names and the wedding date on the front looks stylish and elegant. For a contemporary wedding, you can be more adventurous and add decorative touches that reflect the theme of the day. If the weather on your wedding day is likely to be hot, providing an order of service that can double as a fan will be most welcome.

The wording for the order of service usually includes the wedding location, the time and date, the names of the couple and the celebrant, all the words for each of the hymns (if you are having any),

OPPOSITE The order of service allows guests to follow each stage of proceedings. It is usual to include the words to hymns for a religious ceremony and the names of speakers along with the source of their readings. The service sheets can be placed on each seat, handed out by ushers as guests arrive, or displayed in a basket close to the entrance for guests to help themselves.

BELOW At an outdoor event, the order of service is given a quirky and original touch by attaching the simple card to a child's ice-lolly stick and tying a white ribbon around the stick. The sticks are placed in a wicker basket and offered to guests as they arrive for the ceremony. On a hot summer's day the cards double as fans so people can keep cool in the sunshine.

details of the readings and the names of those giving the readings, plus the name of the organist if applicable.

The order of service is a useful document but very personal, so feel free to include special tributes to absent, perhaps deceased, relatives and thank-yous for special friends who have contributed in some extra way to your day.

As with all other stationery, it is crucial to check and double-check the wording before approving the text for printing. Order enough sheets to allow one for each guest plus an additional 20 copies for unexpected people who may come along to the ceremony to wish you well.

RECEPTION STATIONERY

While none of the following items is an essential part of your wedding, all of them help to make your guests feel welcome at your celebration and to find their seats. Ask your stationery company to prepare these items as part of the stationery order or make simple versions on a computer yourself.

table plan

A table plan – indispensable at larger celebrations – should be displayed just outside the entrance to the dining room, mounted on a board and set up on an artist's easel. Guests will congregate in this area for drinks and should be encouraged to check where they are sitting during the cocktail hour.

   The print on the table plan needs to be large enough to allow guests to see their names easily. Write the name or number of each table followed by a list of the people to be seated at that table or, alternatively, list everyone in alphabetical order with their table name or number next to their name.

escort cards

An alternative to a table plan is to use escort cards. Each guest will have a card or envelope bearing their name with their table name or number written on the reverse. These are arranged in alphabetical order on a decorated table; this should be sited somewhere close to the dining-room entrance. For an additional 'wow' element, each card can be threaded with ribbon and hung from an 'escort tree'.

RIGHT A towering display of escort cards, each threaded onto ribbon and hung from 'tree' branches, makes a spectacular addition to a reception entrance. Leave scissors for guests to use since tugging them off may cause the tree to topple over!

place or seating cards

Once your guests have found their allocated tables, they will be pleased to see their names on cards resting on their plates. These can be simple flat cards, tented cards or labels attached to favours.

menu

Your guests will want to know what they can expect to eat, so a menu card will also be welcome. Either allocate one menu per guest or have one larger menu placed in the centre of the table. The menu card should indicate any vegetarian options and give the name and vintage of each of the wines you have chosen.

wishing tree

A similar idea to the escort tree is a 'wishing tree', which gives guests the chance to send messages of good luck to the couple. The messages are written onto little cards pre-threaded with ribbon that are then tied onto branches of twisted willow displayed in a large vase to make an impressive centrepiece. After the wedding the cards are collected and pasted into an album as a lasting memento. An alternative is to have a guest book displayed near the door to the dining room, where everyone should be encouraged to write messages.

thank-you cards

Your guests will expect to receive thank-you cards for their wedding presents. Thank-you cards can either be sent out as and when you receive each gift or you can do them all in one go after you return from your honeymoon.

To personalize a thank-you note, try to mention the gift and give some indication of how it might be used – for example, 'We loved the toaster and I look forward to [husband's name] serving me many fine breakfasts in bed.' It is satisfying to reflect the style used for other wedding stationery by having thank-you cards that incorporate the same design as that used on the other paper items. Or you might like to have one of your favourite wedding pictures turned into a simple card.

It is important to write your thank-you cards by hand (a printed card is not considered polite), but bear in mind that nobody expects a work of art; just a few heartfelt words of appreciation are fine.

BELOW LEFT Place cards can be simple white cards or, for a more formal touch, put each card in a colour-coordinated envelope and display it on a napkin.

BELOW Everyone likes to know what they will be eating, so, to whet the appetite, prepare menus listing the various dishes and accompanying wines.

floral expressions

If anything comes close to rivalling
the beauty of the bride, it is the beauty
of the wedding flowers. A wedding
wouldn't be a wedding without
fabulous flowers – and they are the
wedding stylist's secret weapon for
creating instant impact and adding a
delicious fragrance to any venue.

floral expressions

Flowers are an integral part of any wedding and, even if you are on a small budget, you should be able to incorporate splashes of colour into all the different elements of the day. Remember that less is more, and clever styling will go a long way towards convincing guests that your displays include lots of flowers when it's more about positioning and using inexpensive foliage.

There are no right or wrong choices when it comes to the perfect flowers for your wedding. You may think you haven't a clue what you want, but peruse a few magazines and you'll soon start to get a feel for the colours and shapes that appeal to you most. You will have to consider the time of year if you want to get the most from your budget, and the style of the venue and the wedding theme will be key factors in leading you in the right direction. Once you have done some initial research, you can step inside any flower shop and discover a rainbow of colours and a myriad of exciting varieties waiting to tempt you.

You need to choose a florist who shares your vision so that you can work together to create a stylish celebration. On a practical note, it's a good idea to visit possible florists during the week rather than on Saturdays, when they are likely to be busy and you're less likely to get their full attention. You are bound to have some ideas before a first visit, so put together some images from magazines of flowers you like. Don't worry if you don't know what the flowers are called, or even if they are in season; these cuttings will be invaluable in indicating to the florist what type of look you're after. Take along a picture of your venue, and a shot of your wedding dress if available, to create as clear a picture as possible of the size and style of the event you are planning.

OPPOSITE A stunning bridal bouquet of blush roses has had all the foliage removed to create a classically elegant display.

RIGHT A simple idea for a modern ceremony is to attach small buckets of flowers to the end of each pew. This mixture of peonies and hydrangeas looks fresh and pretty.

trade secret

'The most important thing to think about when choosing your bouquet is the style and shape of your wedding dress. Many brides focus on their reception theme, but the ceremony flowers can be completely different in colour and design. Talk to your florist — you don't want something too ornate to drown a simple gown or a small posy to disappear in front of a full-skirted dress. When it comes to the type of flowers, the best are those that won't wilt too quickly and have a delicate scent to accompany you down the aisle.'

Kate Smallwood, *Wedding Flowers* magazine

what to ask a potential florist

* have you worked at my venues before?
* will you be doing my flowers or will it be one of your other florists?
* do you have a portfolio showing previous weddings?
* what will be in season for my wedding?
* what style of bouquet will work with my wedding dress?
* what style of centrepieces will suit my venue and my budget?
* what happens if the flowers I order are unavailable on the day?
* can you provide vases, candelabra, etc.? will they cost extra?
* do we pay a deposit? when is the balance due?
* what is your cancellation policy?

WHAT FLOWERS DO YOU NEED?

First of all, think about the setting for the wedding and how formal the occasion will be. If you are planning a casual garden reception, it is probably unnecessary to have a large number of formal arrangements, and a smattering of large vases brimming with sunflowers and dahlias will look stylish and appropriate. On the other hand, a formal sit-down dinner indoors demands that each table should have some kind of floral centrepiece, with more formal arrangements at the entrance and perhaps on the cake table too. A blank canvas such as a white marquee will also benefit from the splashes of colour that flowers can provide.

Make a list of all the areas in your chosen venues where you would ideally like to include some flowers. Try to imagine the role that flowers will play at each stage of the day; think of the ceremony room, reception venue, your bouquet, your bridesmaids' flowers, buttonholes/boutonnieres and other accessories. Write down your ideal flower requirements for each part of the day so you will be well prepared to discuss ideas with your florist.

CEREMONY FLOWERS

If you are marrying in a church, you can either use the services of the church florist or ask your own florist to provide the decorations. Find out whether there is another wedding planned for the same day; if there is, speak to the other couple to see if you can share the cost of decorating the church.

If you are marrying outside the UK, you can exchange vows in the open air, which is a popular choice for many couples. Think about creating a focal point for the ceremony – a decorated bridal arch or arbour are favourite ideas, and these can be hired cheaply then decorated by your florist.

If you are having a Jewish wedding ceremony, you will be married beneath a *chuppah*. This often incorporates an heirloom *tallit* (shawl) or fabric with special meaning – for example, a piece taken from a mother's wedding gown.

For all styles of ceremony, concentrate your budget on where your guests' eyes will be focused. A pedestal arrangement on either side of the altar is usual and, if your budget allows, a small floral arrangement at the end of each pew is a pretty way to welcome guests to their seats. For an outdoor ceremony, where you will be hiring the seats, think about adding colour-coordinated cushions and make a 'carpet' of fresh petals on the grass to create an aisle for the bride to make her entrance.

LEFT If your ceremony is being held in an ornate church, you'll need to invest in larger floral arrangements to make an impact. Sprays of roses with an abundance of foliage arranged around a candelabra are ideal for either side of the altar.

OPPOSITE, LEFT Decorations need not be complex. These hydrangeas tied to alternate pew ends with bright-red ribbon look stylish and welcoming.

OPPOSITE, RIGHT For an outdoor ceremony, each row of chairs is decorated with a small summer posy and arranged on a twisted willow 'stand'.

Decorating the entrance to the church makes sense since this is where many of the photographs will be taken. Potted bay trees adorned with an abundance of white ribbon look effective on either side of the door, or you can ask your florist about creating an arch out of twisted twigs that can be dotted with bows or single flowers. Providing paper cones of fresh petals for guests to use as confetti is another idea you may like to consider, particularly if your venue bans paper confetti or rice.

If you are planning a relatively informal, civil wedding, you will still want to decorate the area where you say your vows. At the simplest civil ceremony at a register office or town hall, you will sit in front of a desk that may or may not already have some kind of flower arrangement. This type of ceremony is over quite quickly, so you may not feel it's a good use of your budget to spend a lot to brighten what can be a fairly plain room. Among the possibilities are a pedestal arrangement on either side of the table and small posies attached to the back of the chairs where the bride and groom will be sitting.

If your ceremony and reception are being held at a single location, speak to your florist or venue manager about moving any flower displays from the ceremony area after the ceremony is over and using them to decorate the reception area.

RECEPTION FLOWERS

At your reception, first impressions count, so make sure the entrance to the dining room is welcoming, drawing your guests inside. This is the ideal place for an impressive pedestal or a floral door wreath, perhaps incorporating ribbon bearing your names and the wedding date.

When your guests step inside the dining room or marquee/tent for the first time, you want them to think 'Wow!' Nothing will more reliably produce this effect than beautiful flowers on each table. Centrepieces should be low, no more than 25cm (10in) high, so your guests can talk over them, or in tall vases so that they can talk under them. In a smaller room it is usual to keep the centrepieces the same, but if you have a lot of tables you can alternate between low and tall arrangements to avoid an overall effect that is too uniform. Make sure the containers you use are also well suited to the style of the room. Glass vases look good in a more contemporary setting; silverware works in a formal dining room; and anything rustic such as terracotta is best kept for an outdoor setting or an occasion such as a picnic or barn dance.

For a more eclectic style, each table can be given its own theme and the flowers chosen to

ABOVE LEFT AND RIGHT If you are using a clear container for a centrepiece, consider how to add interest, so your guests have more to look at than just stems and water. The vase on the left has been filled with grapes to match the vibrant green of the foliage. For the one on the right, clear bubble-filled gel is used instead of water to keep the flowers fresh.

BELOW Work with your florist to create the most eye-catching centrepieces. Flowers should match your colour scheme but don't forget the containers. Most florists have a wide range of vases as well as more ornate holders such as candelabra to hire. Here, spectacular red roses are arranged in gilt candelabra to match the gold chairs.

trade secret

'If you are working to a tight budget, aim to create maximum impact. One fabulous large display strategically placed will give you more of a wow! factor and be more memorable than lots of smaller arrangements. When it comes to colour, keep it simple. Go for blocks of vibrant colour or tones of one shade.'

Nikki Tibbles, Wild At Heart florist

essential flowers

* bridal bouquet
* groom's buttonhole/boutonniere
* bridesmaids' posies
* altar or ceremony arrangement
* table centrepieces
* thank-you bouquets

... if budget allows

* guest buttonholes/corsages
* pew ends
* church entrance
* petal confetti
* reception entrance/hallways
* fireplace
* mantelpiece
* cake table

LEFT If you can afford it, a line-up of tall vases alternating with low arrangements will impress your guests sitting on banquet-style tables.

BELOW It's a nice touch to decorate the backs of some of the guest chairs. You could do this for all female guests or just the bride and groom.

reflect this, in which case every arrangement could end up quite different. This can look stunning and highly individual but be careful not to introduce too many colours or the effect will be jarring on the eye.

You also may like to think about using flowers for place markers on the tables. Tie a simple name tag on to the stem of a single flower, or tie a small posy onto the back of each chair to welcome your guests to their seats. Fresh flowers may also be used to decorate your cake – arranged on top or to separate the various tiers.

It is usual for the groom, during his speech, to give bouquets to the mother of the bride and his own mother, and to anyone who has contributed to the wedding in a special way – for instance, did a friend or relative make the cake?

COLOURS SCHEMES

Your main aim when selecting wedding flowers is to choose something you like. But you also want to create an atmosphere of relaxation and harmony that lasts throughout the day, so the décor and the flowers need to work together. Sunflowers, for example, may be your favourite flower but their overblown simplicity would look completely out of place in a stately home. Delicate pastel-pink roses look gorgeous against the backdrop of a white marquee/tent but would be lost inside a room with a heavily patterned carpet and brocade curtains.

That is why it is important to work with a florist who has either done a previous wedding at your venue, or at least visited the venue, so he or she can make appropriate recommendations.

The simplest solution to choosing your flowers is to go with the season. This will also help your budget since abundant seasonal flowers will be cheaper than imported or specially grown flowers that are not usually available at that time of the year. Spring and summer weddings work best with pastel flowers and plenty of white. A wedding that takes place in autumn/fall or winter, when it's likely

ABOVE The bride's and maids' flowers do not have to match. The theme for these posies is purple and lilac, but each one has different highlights of cream, peach and yellow.

OPPOSITE, ABOVE A bridal bouquet suitable for an autumn or a winter wedding features a glorious mix of Black Baccara roses, orange tulips, orchids and shiny green leaves.

OPPOSITE, BELOW White bouquets look stylish all year round. Here the florist has combined chrysanthemums and orchids to great effect.

to be dark outside, allows you to choose brighter, bolder colours. Ask your florist about incorporating colour in the form of beads, feathers and other fabrics in the table arrangements and your bouquet. This is currently very popular and works particularly well with a contemporary theme.

seasonal colour

spring

pastel pink and white

lemon yellow and white

lilac and white

summer

yellow and mint green

cool white

tiffany blue and silver

autumn/fall

orange and gold

purple and green

gold and cream

winter

ice white

silver and white

red and rich green

trade secret

'Beautiful weddings can be afforded on any budget; the key is to be realistic about what you can achieve. Start by deciding which flowers are essential, then move on to your "wish list". That way, you can keep your needs and desires in perspective. A sensible benchmark is to spend approximately the same on the flowers as you do on your dress.'

Paula Pryke, florist

FLOWERS ON A BUDGET

Creating a floral extravaganza is easy if you have lots of money, but if you don't have much to spend you shouldn't have to compromise on style – you just need to be a little more creative. Be honest with your florist from day one about your budget so he or she knows what is available to work with.

The obvious way to save money is to have fewer flowers and to do without ornate table arrangements that may involve wiring individual flowers, which is very time-consuming and therefore costly. If there is a particular but expensive flower that you love, use it sparingly – perhaps only in your bridal bouquet, making it doubly special and even more memorable.

There is nothing to say that your flowers all have to be the same; providing the overall colour scheme works, you should feel free to mix and

match. Do not dismiss 'common' flowers either, since these can look stunning in the hands of a good florist. Carnations, tulips, gypsophila and daffodils are all cheap and look impressive when massed together in large vases.

Surprisingly few flowers are needed to make a visual statement and fill a room with fragrance. Ask your florist about using lilies, hyacinths, frangipani, apple and orange blossom, mimosa, stocks, jasmine and sweet peas in some of the reception arrangements. All of these have a beautiful scent.

Don't be misled into thinking it is necessary to cover every surface with flowers. Frequently, less is more, and a few tall, striking arrangements, well placed where your guests will see them, are more effective than a mass of smaller arrangements on each table. Be creative with colour and fill tall glass vases with coloured stones or citrus fruits and simply put a row of flowers right at the top. Flowering plants in brightly coloured pots arranged in a line or a circle on each table is another pretty idea, and these can double as favours for your guests to take home with them.

ABOVE LEFT If you want a modern feel for your reception tables, simplicity is the key. Here a simple vase is filled with a stunning display of arum lilies and highlighted with votive candles in frosted-glass holders.

LEFT Empty glass bottles are a cheap and effective substitute for vases. Use in quantity, lining them close together on tables or window ledges. Long-stemmed roses work best for this look and are less likely to wilt than many other flower varieties.

year-round favourites

calla lily

carnation

gypsophila

orchid

protea

rose

tulip

favourite flowers in colour

white	sweet pea, rose, stephanotis, camellia, narcissus, orchid, lily of the valley, gardenia, jasmine, gypsolphila
pink	peony, rose, ranunculus, lily, sweet pea, carnation, tulip, protea
lavender	lavender, lilac, delphinium, anemone, statice, iris, hydrangea
yellow	sunflower, lily, tulip, gerbera, daffodil, freesia
red	rose, gerbera, dahlia, poinsettia, amaryllis

ABOVE LEFT For an outdoor wedding, ask your florist about using potted plants rather than flower arrangements to decorate tables. This wooden slatted container of grass surrounded by tea lights works perfectly at a beach reception.

LEFT This bride wanted a minimalist bouquet to match her simple, slim dress, so the florist bound together long-stemmed white tulips using a dark green fabric fixed with pearl-topped pins.

FAR LEFT Fill a wide, low glass bowl with water, add a sprinkling of fresh rose petals and a few floating candles and you've got a centrepiece that anyone can afford.

THE BRIDE'S BOUQUET

The bouquet is the ultimate wedding accessory, the options being limited only by the availability of the flowers, the skill of the florist – and the bride's imagination. The style of the wedding and the shape of your dress will guide you towards the perfect bouquet.

To make sure you achieve the right balance between your dress and the flowers, do not finalize your bouquet until after you have chosen your outfit. There are no hard and fast rules but, in general terms, the bigger the dress the bigger the bouquet. An oversized bouquet of trailing lilies, for example, could overpower a simple or slinky dress, while a tiny, delicate posy would look unbalanced if you are wearing a full-skirted ball gown. To help your florist come up with appropriate suggestions, take a picture or at least a sketch of your dress along with you when you meet the florist for the first time.

Keeping the bouquet looking fresh can be a worry, especially in hot summer weather. Try to handle it as little as possible once it arrives, leaving it nestled in tissue paper and out of direct sunlight. Contrary to popular belief, you shouldn't put your bouquet in the fridge since flowers do not like any extremes of temperature. Just as you are about to leave for the ceremony, pinch out any bruised petals and gently fluff out the edges, which may have got flattened in transit. Always hold the bouquet slightly away from your body to avoid crushing the flowers or marking your dress.

ABOVE A tightly packed bunch of deep red roses makes the perfect bridal bouquet. A collar of trailing ivy adds extra colour.

RIGHT A cascade of tiny orchids threaded onto wire is allowed to 'float' around the main bouquet, a tropical mix of calla lilies and orchids.

OPPOSITE This classic posy of cream roses and cream calla lilies has stems bound together with cream satin ribbon to match the gown decoration.

LEFT The addition of lilac hydrangeas to this hand-tied posy of cream roses makes it ideal for an autumn/fall bride.

styles of bouquet

hand-tied Flowers such as roses are wired together or casually hand-tied. They work best at a contemporary wedding with a modern, simple dress.

pomander A tight ball of flowers such as carnations, usually without any foliage, are suspended on a ribbon that the bride can hang from her wrist.

posy Small, simple and usually hand-tied with ribbon. Lily of the valley makes the perfect minimalist posy.

round The classic bouquet, usually consisting of larger flowers such as roses and peonies that are loosely arranged with foliage and tied with ribbon.

shower A waterfall-like spill of flowers wired to cascade from a handle. This is the most traditional and formal of the bouquet shapes and suits full-skirted dresses.

BRIDESMAIDS' FLOWERS

The bridesmaids' flowers should reflect the style and colour of the bride's bouquet. The most popular option is to give each bridesmaid an identical posy, which can be a smaller version of the bridal bouquet or something completely different. Alternatively, each maid can carry a posy of her favourite flowers, but all of these should come from the same colour family. As long as the effect is well coordinated, you should be pleased with the result.

Younger flower girls often enjoy carrying a small basket filled with flowers or fresh petals to scatter down the aisle. If you don't want them to have to carry anything, ask your florist to design a floral bracelet or pretty hair decoration so they still feel special. For the under-fives, a teddy bear wearing a fresh corsage is a sweet alternative and doubles as a thank-you gift.

BUTTONHOLES/BOUTONNIERES AND CORSAGES

The groom and the main male members of the bridal party will usually wear buttonholes/boutonnieres. This looks appropriate to the occasion and helps to tie together the whole wedding party. Popular flowers for buttonholes/boutonnieres include roses, orchids, carnations and smaller varieties of lily. Your groom will probably want to wear something slightly different from his best man and ushers, ideally a flower that is being used in your bouquet. Many couples leave a tray of buttonholes/boutonnieres at the door of the ceremony for guests to help themselves. It is also a nice idea to give the fathers of the bride and groom a special buttonhole/boutonniere, and both mothers a corsage (make sure they complement their outfits). Popular corsage flowers include roses, orchids, gardenias and camellias.

ABOVE For a summer wedding, bridesmaids wear hairbands made from wired fresh flowers, decorated with twists of organza ribbon to match their dresses.

OPPOSITE, ABOVE Flower girls can be given baskets of fresh petals to carry and scatter along the aisle before the bride makes her entrance.

OPPOSITE, BELOW To reflect a green and orange scheme, two adult bridesmaids carry posies of shamrock chrysanthemums, red and orange roses, lime-green orchids and orange calla lilies.

BELOW Pink peonies look equally stunning when tightly budded and fully open, as in this bridesmaid's posy.

ABOVE A classic combination for a wedding buttonhole/boutonniere is rose and ivy. A romantically minded groom will usually choose to replicate in his buttonhole/boutonniere the same variety of flower as used in his bride's bouquet.

LEFT Since it is expensive, lily of the valley is generally used only in small quantities at weddings, but it can make eye-catching and sweetly scented buttonholes/boutonnieres for the groom and his best man.

CLASSIC WEDDING BLOOMS

rose

The rose is the most popular and versatile of all the wedding flowers and is available in hundreds of different varieties and colours to suit every colour scheme. Hybrid roses are long-lasting and grown all year round but have little scent. For a delicious fragrance, choose old-fashioned roses that evoke all the delights of the garden on a summer's day.

peony

With their lush, overblown flowers in white or all shades of pink, peonies are a favourite among summer brides. The flowers are quite large, so they look most dramatic when used on their own in a hand-held bouquet or as part of a stunning table centrepiece.

lily of the valley

Loved for its tiny bell-shaped flowers and heavenly scent, lily of the valley is very popular with spring brides. It can be used on its own in a posy or mixed with other flowers such as garden roses or sweet peas. The delicate nature of the flowers and the short growing season means it is very expensive and usually seen only in small quantities.

hydrangea

For a casual and very romantic feel, hydrangeas look beautiful as part of a bouquet or reception arrangement. The characteristic round, blossom-like heads come in a variety of colours, but purple, pink or white are the most popular for weddings. Mix with lilacs, delphiniums or anemones in contrasting shades.

orchid

Wonderfully seductive-looking flowers with more than a touch of the exotic, orchids are available in many varieties and a wide range of colours from white to vibrant pink. Cymbidium and phalaenopsis orchids are popular for bouquets and modern table arrangements. Spray orchids, which have smaller flowers, are mixed with other flowers for bouquets and centrepieces.

calla lily

Modern brides love calla lilies because of their bold colours and sleek shape. Simply tied together, they make a statement bouquet for a contemporary wedding that can be stylishly nestled in the crook of your arm. They are available in a wide variety of colours from brilliant yellow to red and purple.

FLOWERS FOR EVERY SEASON

SPRING

amaryllis A large, open flower available in pure white to brightest red. Perfect for larger bouquets and centrepieces.

anemone Characterized by its coloured centre; available in more than 100 varieties. The brighter colours are wonderful for trendy posies.

daffodil A bright and cheerful yellow flower that is always popular for spring weddings.

freesia Small, highly scented flowers in bright colours. Ideal for headdresses and posies.

gerbera Large and dramatic daisy-like flowers that come in orange, red, pink and yellow.

lily of the valley Tiny, bell-shaped white flowers with a sweet fragrance. A classic wedding flower and ideal for small posies. Expensive.

orchid Exotic and expensive but available in a variety of pretty colours. Just a few long stems simply tied make a fabulous modern bouquet.

ranunculus A buttercup-shaped flower popular for spring weddings. Available in a variety of colours.

stephanotis A popular wedding flower famed for its small white wedding blooms and sweet scent.

sweet pea A classic wedding favourite with delicate petals and a sweet, lingering fragrance.

ABOVE The tightly packed beauty of the ranunculus makes it popular as an addition to many spring bridal bouquets.

LEFT Lily of the valley has long been a favourite with spring brides and is loved for its delicate bell-shaped flowers and amazing fragrance.

SUMMER

anthurium Famous for its glossy, waxy-looking flowers. Popular for beach and tropical themes.

carnation A traditional choice for a buttonhole/boutonniere and available in lots of colours. Also works well en masse for table arrangements.

chrysanthemum A versatile flower ranging from daisy-like flowers to large pompom shapes. Available in a wide variety of colours.

gypsophila Tiny white or pink flowers also known as Baby's Breath. Best used in quantity to form a cloud-like display or as an accent flower.

lily There are about a hundred varieties in a huge range of colours. Colourful calla lilies or large white arum lilies are two wedding favourites.

magnolia Large, subtly scented flowers in a wide range of shapes and colours. Popular for reception decoration.

peony Large, fragrant flowers with petals in a bowl shape. A popular bouquet or centrepiece flower, available in pink, white, magenta and yellow.

rose The most popular of all the wedding flowers and used for bouquets and decorations. Available in a wide variety of sizes, varieties and colours. Choose garden roses for their scent.

sunflower A refreshing choice for a summer wedding. They can be pricey but are so big you won't need many to make a visual impact.

ABOVE Posies of peach calla lilies are bound with colour-coordinated peach fabric and secured with pearl-tipped pins.

RIGHT For a contemporary table arrangement, cover a small glass cube vase with strips of bright orange material and then add a selection of tightly budded roses to match the colour scheme.

AUTUMN/FALL

agapanthus Large balls of bell-shaped flowers in a striking shade of violet or blue. They add a splash of colour to bouquets and centrepieces.

aster Small, daisy-like flower in a variety of colours, usually with a bright yellow centre. Pretty in bouquets.

clematis Perfect for trailing bouquets. Available in a good selection of sizes and colours.

daisy An all-year-round favourite that always looks bright and cheerful. An ideal flower on which to theme your whole wedding.

hosta Not strictly a flower but a variety of popular foliage with heart-shaped leaves ranging in colour from soft to brilliant green; often variegated.

hydrangea Large, romantic flowerheads in a variety of pretty pastel colours. Good for centrepieces and pedestal arrangements.

passion flower Large, exotic flowers that can be used to add splashes of bright colour to a bouquet or centrepiece.

pinks Available in white and, not surprisingly, a variety of tones of pink – from very pale to almost red. Pretty round flowers ideal for bouquets.

LEFT Take every opportunity to make your guests feel welcome at the reception. Here, a table of escort cards is adorned by a large stone vase overflowing with a beautiful mixture of white hydrangeas, cream roses, twisted willow and eucalyptus leaves.

WINTER

camellia Beautiful open-faced flowers ranging from a single row of petals to overlapping multi-rows. Popular for buttonholes/boutonnieres because of their richly coloured and shiny foliage.

euphorbia An evergreen shrub with yellowish flowers. Useful as an all-year-round addition to venue displays and more elaborate bouquets.

iris An unusual fan-shaped flower with three large petals. Usually lilac, purple or white and popular for centrepieces.

nerine Sprays of hot or pale pink trumpet-shaped flowers. Fairly exotic, so good for unusual centrepieces.

pansy Small, flat-faced flowers in a variety of colours and intensities. Plants can be kept in their pots and double as table decorations and pretty favours.

poinsettia Not strictly a flower, this Christmas favourite is perfect for adding a festive flavour to your reception. Grown in pots; can be small or grow to several feet tall. Classic red is the most popular but the white variety is equally effective.

snowdrop A delicate white flower and one of the classic bridal blooms. Ideal in hand-tied posies and for smaller table decorations.

tulip A cheerful favourite available in a wide variety of colours. The varieties with frilled edges are very popular for contemporary bouquets.

BELOW This pretty posy of pansies and forget-me-nots has a matching collar of purple ribbon.

BOTTOM Peonies are a popular wedding flower and look stunning grouped in vases for centrepieces. A cost effective option since you don't need any other flowers to achieve a great effect.

The meaning of flowers

Flowers are said to have a language all their own. Find out what secret messages you will be sending to your groom through the flowers you choose for your bouquet.

apple blossom	**perfection**
arum lily	**ardour**
azalea	**true to the end**
bluebell	**lasting love**
camellia	**perfect loveliness**
carnation (red)	**admiration**
carnation (white)	**sweet and lovely**
daffodil	**joy**
daisy	**innocence**
forget-me-not	**true love**
freesia	**sweetness**
gardenia	**purity and joy**
gerbera	**cheerfulness**
honeysuckle	**bonds of love**
iris	**hope and wisdom**
jasmine	**sensuality**
lemon blossom	**fidelity**
lily of the valley	**happiness**
mimosa	**sensitivity**
orchid	**beauty**
rose (pink)	**happiness**
rose (red)	**I love you**
rose (white)	**purity**
snowdrop	**hope**
stephanotis	**marital happiness**
sunflower	**adoration**
sweet pea	**lasting pleasure**
tulip (red)	**love**
tulip (yellow)	**sunshine of my life**
violet	**faithfulness**

RIGHT A large venue demands impressive table centres such as this white candelabrum covered with an arrangement of cream roses, various shades of hydrangea and twists of bells of Ireland. The centrepiece is ringed with smaller vases of the same flowers to dramatic effect.

reception style

Being faced with an empty function
room and having the vision to transform
it into a celebration that encapsulates
a dream is quite a challenge for
a professional, let alone for someone
who has never planned anything more
complex than a family meal before.
But it can be done.

reception style

Planning a successful wedding is all about good communication – articulating what's inside your head so the people around you can understand what's required and then make it happen, on time and on budget. Rather than trying to go it alone, it makes sense to surround yourself with a team of professionals, from the venue manager to your photographer – people who fill you with confidence and who you trust to deliver your dream.

At most wedding locations, your team will be led by the on-site wedding coordinator or the hospitality manager. This should be the person you met when first viewing the venue and someone with whom you feel at ease, confident that they understand and share your vision down to the smallest detail. The coordinator or manager will be your contact throughout the planning process and should be available to answer your questions and to provide advice as the big day gets closer.

When it comes to selecting other members of the team, ask the venue staff for recommendations of suppliers they have worked with in the past. Many larger venues have an on-site florist or a contract with a local florist to provide flowers for big occasions such as weddings. This doesn't mean that you are obliged to use their services, but working with someone who knows your venue and the staff has its advantages. Find out which photographers have worked at your venue before and, when you visit them, ask to see shots from those weddings. Seeing how other people decorated your venue, as well as where they had their pictures taken, offers invaluable insight into what worked – and what didn't work so well.

OPPOSITE A marquee/tent with open sides is ideal for a summer garden wedding when you want to give the feeling of being outdoors without having to worry about bad weather.

RIGHT If you want to create an elegant mood, it is hard to go wrong with a classic colour combination such as yellow, gold and white.

HIRING PROFESSIONAL HELP

If your time is limited by work commitments or you know you are not very good at managing people and will struggle to give instructions or deal with tricky situations, consider employing a professional wedding planner. A professional can either be involved only with key decisions such as finding a venue or hold your hand through every stage, effectively acting as the client when dealing with suppliers. You make the decisions and the planner will make sure it happens. Most wedding planners have a wonderful eye for decoration and style and will be able to make plenty of creative suggestions about how to make the most efficient use of your space. They should also have excellent contacts with other suppliers such as florists, caterers and photographers and be able to make suitable recommendations.

Wedding organizers charge either a percentage of the total cost of the wedding or a set fee for a set amount of time. What they save you in stress could well be worth their fee many times over.

you need a wedding planner if ...

* you have a hectic lifestyle and little spare time
* you have no close family or friends to help you
* you are using a venue a long way from where you live, or abroad
* you are terrified by the thought of managing suppliers
* you haven't got a clue where to start, with anything at all

TOP Eye-catching centrepieces, such as this tall vase brimming with white flowers, will always look most impressive in a large room with plenty of tables.

RIGHT This spectacular contemporary marquee/tent needed little decoration other than the strings of fairy lights in the ceiling.

CREATING THE RIGHT ATMOSPHERE

If you get the atmosphere at your reception just right, your guests will feel both welcome and relaxed from the moment they arrive. Your venue, and the staff, will play a big part in promoting the right mood. Even if your venue is formal, there is no reason why staff should be stuffy or standoffish. A friendly smile and a helpful attitude are prerequisites at any location. Your guests will feel more at ease if greeted by soft background music rather than silence as they enter any room. Brief any bridesmaids and ushers to circulate and make sure that nobody is left standing on their own.

Lighting also plays an important role in creating a relaxing atmosphere. Many function rooms have a dual role, being used for business meetings during the week and for weddings and parties at the weekend. The kind of lighting that works for a conference is unlikely to be appropriate for a wedding reception, so you need to make sure that you check the quality and flexibility of the lighting well in advance of the big day. Ask to see the room with all the lights on to gauge how bright it feels. Most overhead lighting is too harsh for a wedding so, hopefully, your venue has dimmer switches and side lighting that can be used instead to cast a warm glow around the room. It may also be possible to change the wattage of the light bulbs.

Think about the time of year and time of day you will be using the rooms. You may be viewing the location during the summer while the wedding is due to take place in the autumn, by which time the quality of the natural light will

TOP If your venue needs to look welcoming and elegant into the evening, you can use candlelight – in this case, lanterns – to create a romantic atmosphere.

ABOVE Try to view potential reception venues at the time of day you will be using them so that you can make sure the lighting evokes the right mood.

trade secret

'Use intelligent lighting to put together a customized assortment of lights that can be alternated through the night. Options include an "excitement" palette of reds and oranges to energize your guests and a calming "in-between-courses" palette of blues and purples, which can soothe guests and facilitate conversation.'

Bentley Meeker, New York lighting expert

be completely different. The pretty room that had sunlight streaming through the windows when you saw it on a summer morning could well be gloomy by the late afternoon at the time of year when you will be holding your reception there.

If the lighting doesn't feel right and cannot be altered, you may need to consider adding extra lights of your own. It is a good idea to employ a lighting specialist who will know exactly what to use and where to place any extra lighting to best effect. You can hire spotlights and uplighters to position around the room, and candles on each table are essential. Candelabra make stunning centrepieces and you can work with your florist to incorporate these into your floral arrangements. For a less formal look, tea lights/votives are inexpensive and when used in large numbers cast a romantic light over a table. Cluster them around a floral centrepiece or use them on their own to give

a minimalist look to your tables. Some historical houses do not allow naked flame, so you won't be able to have candles in such venues, although lanterns may be acceptable, as long as the flame is covered. Alternatively, you can buy battery-powered lights, including tea lights, that give a flame-effect and last for anything up to ten hours.

If you are having a summer wedding and using outdoor space, you need to think about how it will look after dark. Tree branches can be strung with fairy lights or a trail of paper lanterns, pathways can be lined with flaming torches and patios ringed with Moroccan-style lanterns. At one memorable wedding, the couple covered the lawn in front of their venue with more than 1,000 tea lights/votives – time-consuming to do but a definite wow! factor for all the guests.

LEFT For an evening reception at this imposing venue, the overhead lighting is dimmed; atmospheric lighting is provided by candles on the tables and spotlights in the alcoves.

OPPOSITE The professional who styled this wedding created a romantic mood with a line of potted trees the length of the ballroom, each lit with hundreds of twinkling fairy lights.

day into night
As night falls, you will probably want to create a romantic mood.
* Dim light switches or turn off 50 per cent of room lighting.
* Light candles on tables, mantelpieces and window ledges.
* Weather permitting, put lanterns and torches on patios to draw guests outside.
* Illuminate the dance floor and turn off lighting at the edges of the room.
* Hang a curtain of fairy lights between the dance floor and seating areas.
* Have your initials spotlit in the middle of the dance floor.

ROOM LAYOUT

If your reception is in a traditional location such as a marquee/tent, a hotel or conference facility, the chances are that the space will be uniform in shape with few breaks in the walls other than windows and doors – in other words, an empty shell that's easy to work with in terms of table layout, although perhaps more challenging if you want to stamp your personal style on the room.

At a more unusual location such as a historical building, a museum or even your own home, the shape of the room where the reception is held is likely to be less uniform, with recesses, staircases, pillars, mantelpieces and larger items of furniture such as bookcases all needing to be taken into account when it comes to where to put your tables.

Learn from the experience of others and, if possible, ask to see pictures of previous events –

not just weddings – for ideas of how the rooms can be styled. Find out how many people are seated in each picture. Does the room look spacious or cramped? A large number of people may fit into a room but, if they are squashed together, it does not make for a relaxed and enjoyable event.

Will the rooms you are thinking about for the reception be in use in the near future for an event that you can view for inspiration? Most venues will be happy for you to take a peek once the room has been set up, and it will be much easier for you to finalize your plans once you have seen a room that is filled with furniture rather than empty.

The ideal room layout will allow all your guests to sit comfortably without their elbows touching the person next to them. There also needs to be enough space between the tables to make getting up easy and to allow any entertainers, such as magicians, to move freely around the room. Elderly or pregnant guests and those with small children are best seated around the edges of the room with easy access to the toilets. And while you want the room to feel spacious, tables shouldn't be so far apart that guests feel isolated from one another and the room looks fragmented.

ABOVE If you are using a marquee/tent company, ask to see pictures from previous weddings and learn from what worked and what didn't before committing yourselves.

LEFT A modern setting, such as this barn, has acquired a fun element from the addition of oversized Chinese lanterns to match the colour scheme.

OPPOSITE A plain room is turned into a frothy extravaganza with the clever use of fabric to cover windows, plain walls and unsightly pillars.

do the maths

A room measuring 10 x 10 metres (33 x 33 feet) gives 100 square metres (more than 1,000 square feet) of space to hold about 200 guests standing, 100 guests seated at round tables and 140 guests at rectangular tables.

Your guests will want to have a clear view of the top table and, ideally, should only have to turn their chairs in order to enjoy the speeches. In reality, some of your guests may have to be seated in alcoves or even adjoining rooms if you are having a big wedding, and may have to bring their chairs into the main room when the speeches are announced. If you are having a children-only table, position this in an alcove since they won't be interested in the speeches and won't mind not being able to see what's going on.

fun with fabric

An uninspiring room can be transformed by the clever use of fabrics to line walls, to separate a large room into smaller areas and to create a tent-like ceiling. You will probably need to get an expert involved since putting them up is tricky. Marquee/tent companies are one of the best sources, providing a selection of decorated fabrics — butterfly-covered ceilings are a favourite as well as black ceilings dotted with tiny lights that look like stars.

ROUND VERSUS RECTANGULAR

A traditional reception layout incorporates a mixture of rectangular and round tables. One arrangement is to have a long top table that will seat the bride, the groom, the parents, the best man and the chief bridesmaid plus a selection of round tables seating between eight and fourteen guests each.

Round tables have the advantage of making it easier for guests to talk to one another and the whole table can be involved in one conversation quite easily. On a rectangular table, guests tend to talk only to the person on either side of them. Round tables are also easier to work with if you have limited space or trying to fit an unusually shaped room.

For wow! factor, and marquees/tents are perfect for this, banquet-style seating on one or more very long tables looks stunning. Long tables are laid end to end so it seems as if you have one enormous table in the centre of the room, with anything up to 100 people sitting at it. Alternatively, you can set out three long tables, each seating 50 guests each. Guests can be accommodated on both sides, so conversation flow is not a problem.

LEFT Simplicity is always chic, and in a contemporary setting a black and white theme is a favourite colour combination that looks cool and modern.

OPPOSITE A warehouse venue is transformed with a tropical theme of hot pink and vibrant orange. An indoor tent-effect was created with metres of shimmering organza that was also used to cover the tables. The fuchsia seat pads match the candles and pink orchids in the centrepieces. Coloured glasses and gold chargers complete the transformation.

THE SEATING PLAN

If you are serving a meal to your guests, assigned seating is vital, and working out who will sit where is one of the major headaches of planning almost every wedding. You and your fiancé need to ensure that the combination of people on each table is right and that you haven't inadvertently seated guests together who can't stand each other.

The simplest way to work out your seating plan is to draw it out on a large piece of paper. Make a list of tables with 10–12 slots for each one and gradually fill them up with names. Once the balance on each table looks about right, think about who should be seated next to one another.

Some couples like to keep family and friends together and others split them up so that they get the chance to meet new people, but it is advisable to sit everyone next to at least one person they know. Work colleagues and groups of people who share similar interests should usually sit together.

table seating capacity

round table diameter	ideal	maximum
1.22 metres/4 feet	7	8
1.52 metres/5 feet	8	10
1.83 metres/6 feet	10	12
2.13 metres/7 feet	12	14

traditional top table

chief bridesmaid/groom's father/bride's mother/ groom/bride/bride's father/groom's mother/best man

the top table if parents are divorced and remarried

stepfather/chief bridesmaid/groom's father/bride's mother/groom/ bride/bride's father/groom's mother/best man/stepmother

name your tables

Rather than numbering your tables, personalize each one and give it a themed name. Suggestions for themes include:

* ✳ romantic cities
* ✳ romantic movies
* ✳ romantic songs
* ✳ famous couples
* ✳ favourite flowers
* ✳ champagne brands or fine wines

seating harmony

▢ do seat family together

▢ do seat work colleagues together

▢ do seat people with similar interests together

▢ don't mix age groups too much

▢ don't seat ex-partners together

▢ don't seat all the 'spare' guests together

Male, female, male, female is the ideal scenario for a balanced table, but uneven numbers may make this impossible, in which case you could ask all the male guests to move two seats to their right between each course to vary the conversation. Common sense dictates that you keep divorced couples and ex-partners away from one another. If your guests include a number of single people who are unlikely to know many people, resist the temptation to put them all together on one table. Think about their interests and try to seat them at tables where you know they will find a common bond with someone else.

Buffet-style receptions mean you can dispense with the seating plan and let all your guests find their own seat and a table of their choice, although, if you want family and friends to sit together, assigned seating is still a good idea.

Once the seating plan has been finalized, you need to make a printed version for display so that everyone can find out where they are sitting. This can be done simply on a computer, although there are many stationery companies who are able to create beautifully printed seating charts in keeping with your theme or colour scheme. These need to be produced several weeks before the wedding and cannot usually be amended, so you will have to get organized early if you follow this route.

If you are having a large number of guests, think about having two printed seating plans. These can be displayed on easels and sited at opposite ends of the room to prevent crowding.

ESCORT CARDS

As an alternative to a reception seating plan, some couples use escort cards. Each guest is assigned an envelope with the appropriate table name or number printed on a card inside. The cards are arranged in alphabetical order on a table close to the dining room. If you want to be creative and introduce a wow! factor, the cards can be threaded onto ribbon and hung from an 'escort tree'. This works best at a smaller wedding, where there is less risk of a large number of people grabbing their cards at the same time and knocking the tree over.

OPPOSITE When devising a seating plan, group families, workmates and guests of similar ages together to achieve table harmony. Try to seat single guests on a table where others may share their interests.

BELOW Place cards are a nice touch to welcome guests to their places at a table. Keep it informal by tying the card to a coffee spoon with a pretty ribbon.

BELOW RIGHT There's nothing to say you can't tie each place card around the stem of a glass.

BELOW FAR RIGHT Place cards can double as favours when attached to attractive potted plants such as this muscari in a miniature galvanized pail.

ABOVE Escort cards, arranged in alphabetical order on a table at the entrance to the reception, can replace a seating plan.

PLACE CARDS

Once the meal has been announced and guests start to make their way to the tables, each table needs to be clearly signed and each place should be marked with a place or name card. At formal weddings the format would be Mr John Smith; for a less formal occasion, it would be John Smith. It's inadvisable to use someone's first name alone, however casual the party, since it is likely that there will be people who share the same name.

TABLE DRESSING

The reception tables are the main source of colour and decoration in the dining room. You should aim to achieve an effect that is well coordinated and easy on the eye, with one or two unexpected touches that will delight your guests.

Traditionally, each table will be dressed using the same linens, cutlery and glasses. Each place setting will be marked with a name card and, if you are providing them, a favour for each guest. It is usual to give each guest a printed menu or, on smaller tables, to have one menu in the centre that lists the food and the accompanying wines. Each table will probably have some kind of centrepiece, either a flower arrangement or, at more formal weddings, silver candelabra.

Take care over the height of your centrepieces; they should either be kept low so guests can talk over them or be high enough so that conversation can still flow underneath them. What you want to avoid is for the centrepiece, however pretty it may be, to block people on one side of the table from talking to people on the other. At a large wedding where there is an abundance of tables,

you can vary the centrepieces from one table to another, alternating the use of low and tall arrangements.

If you are using rectangular tables with guests sitting on either side, line the centre of each table with a row of floral arrangements – one to every four or six guests will usually be enough. If you are on a limited budget, fill the spaces between the centrepieces with rows of tea lights/votives so that all your guests feel their place is special.

The top table seating the main bridal party often has slightly different and more lavish floral arrangements since this table will be the focus of everyone's attention. Any arrangements should be kept low so that guests will have no trouble seeing the bride and groom and anyone who is going to make a speech. It is a lovely idea to decorate the front of the top table with a floral garland tied with ribbon to match the colour theme of the day.

THIS PAGE Napkins offer the perfect opportunity for adding a decorative touch or a splash of colour to the reception table. Traditional cream linens can be folded and tied in any number of imaginative ways and secured with everything from a flower to a twist of gilt wire tipped with pearls. A modern alternative is to hire coloured napkins to match your colour scheme.

OPPOSITE At this Japanese wedding reception, the long top table has been 'attached' to the smaller circular tables by means of ribbons to bring a sense of unification and family harmony to the room.

alternative centrepieces

Get creative and stretch your table-dressing budget.

✳ Fill vases with coloured stones or citrus fruits and top with large flowers.

✳ Theme the centrepieces – for example, you could use buckets of sand with children's windmills for a beach wedding or an arrangement of vintage teacups and roses for an afternoon reception.

✳ Use potted plants in colourful containers that guests can take home as favours.

✳ Ask your florist to use lots of interesting foliage and fewer flowers.

✳ Create a modern centrepiece using large square candles tied with ribbon.

✳ Pile colourful favour boxes into the centre of the table instead of flowers.

✳ Put a piece of mirror under any centrepiece to make it appear bigger.

BELOW You can conceal ugly walls and ceilings by creating an indoor 'room' using swathes of coloured fabric.

RIGHT For a large reception with an abundance of tables, consider alternating tall and short centrepieces on the tables to prevent the room from looking 'samey' and over-coordinated.

OPPOSITE The wedding experience needs to start at the moment people arrive. Welcome guests to the entrance by lining low walls with tea lights/votives or miniature flaming torches.

LESS THAN PERFECT AREAS

Once your reception venue has been decorated, the chances are that less-than-perfect areas will be hardly noticeable, so there is no need to worry about every little detail. What you do have a right to expect is that every part of the venue should be spotlessly clean, there is no peeling paint, and the windows have been recently cleaned, inside and out.

Providing you have included at least one wow! factor in the room, guests will be focused on that and not looking at the ugly light sockets or a fire exit sign resplendent above the door.

If there is any large item that cannot be moved but you would like to be hidden, hire a few trees and create a screen around the offending object. Fire extinguishers are a necessary evil but, with any luck, they will be hidden away in a corner where they won't be noticed.

COMMON PARTS

In your rush to decorate the cocktail location and the dining room, don't forget the other areas your guests will visit. First impressions count, so think about adding a sign of welcome to the front door or the lobby. If you have sole use of the venue, a banner with your names and the wedding date is an appealing idea – or how about a floral wreath to match your colour scheme? At larger venues, you can welcome guests into the rooms you have been assigned by placing potted rose bushes on either side of the entrance, tied with oversize ribbons. You can even extend the welcome into the car park with a wedding signpost signalling where you would like your guests to enter the building.

A sweeping staircase provides a wonderful opportunity for decoration. Trailing ivy through balustrades looks stylish and is a cost-effective way to bring colour to a staid hallway. At a more modern venue, put a lantern containing a lighted candle onto each step and ask the venue manager to ensure the candles get changed halfway through the evening so they are still burning when your guests go home.

Most entrance halls have at least one occasional table and, since this is what your guests will see first, it is worth asking your florist to fill an urn with foliage and large flowers to place on the table and attract people's attention as they arrive.

Last but not least, don't forget the bathrooms. Put a small vase of fresh flowers into each toilet – both the ladies and the gents – along with a basket containing a few essentials such as hairspray, fragrance, tissues and hand cream. At winter weddings, employing an attendant to look after coats and umbrellas is always money well spent.

OUTDOOR SPACES

Anywhere that your guests will see needs to be clean, tidy and welcoming. At a summer wedding, the reception will either be held in the open air or guests will be outside for some part of the day enjoying cocktails or an after-dinner stroll, so terraces and gardens become as important as indoor rooms when thinking about decorations and lighting. At a winter wedding, guests will be using car parks/parking lots and the entrance area, as well as looking out of windows, so it is important that you give them something attractive to see outside as well as inside.

If you have chosen your venue on account of its outside spaces, then it is likely that these will be well maintained and well stocked with flowers, shrubs and trees, so all you have to do is to add the finishing touches.

Since it is risky to depend on good weather, a marquee/tent is an obvious choice for dining and dancing while remaining partly in the open air. If you choose a structure with open sides, this allows guests to enjoy the gardens but provides shelter just in case there's a shower or it gets chilly during the evening.

In high summer, erecting Raj-style or Moroccan tents and filling them with piles of cushions is another popular idea, making a welcome retreat from the hot sun. At the very least, if there is no obviously shaded area, you need to put up some large white garden umbrellas, since standing in direct sun for long quickly becomes uncomfortable for many people. If your venue has a pond, lake or swimming pool you may want to

make a feature of this and set up a dining area close to the water. Floating floral arrangements can look spectacular and the area can be lit by torches or lanterns as night falls.

One word of caution: if you are inviting young children to a wedding reception that includes any areas of water, it is your responsibility to make sure that access is restricted and pools are securely fenced to prevent accidents.

Entertain your guests by setting up seasonal attractions and bring an old-style sense of light-hearted enjoyment to the day. The ultimate fun idea is to hire some fairground rides such as a merry-go-round or dodgem cars. Lesser budgets can stretch to a coconut shy, a candyfloss stall and the two-hour hire of an

ice-cream stall. A game of croquet always goes down well and little ones will love it if you hang a Mexican piñata from a tree.

As night falls, you will want to take full advantage of the outdoor space, so make it welcoming by lining pathways with lit Moroccan lanterns. Citronella torches dotted in shrubs will help to ward off insects. Chinese paper lanterns are very effective to highlight a patio, and you can festoon trees and bushes with inexpensive Christmas lights to transform the darkness into a fairyland. Ask the venue staff to set up a bar on the terrace and arrange to have a guitarist or harpist playing romantic music, at least for the first hour, to encourage guests to go outside.

ABOVE Make the most of an interesting feature, such as a swimming pool, even after dark by highlighting the edges with candles and floating flowers and candles in the water.

ABOVE RIGHT An evening reception in summer lends itself to a spectacular outdoor setting such as this amazing marquee/tent structure that has been outlined with thousands of tiny white lights.

RIGHT Dining outdoors is always popular with guests. This marquee/tent offers the best of both worlds, with a roof but no sides, allowing in the evening breeze. Clever lighting edges the structure and Chinese lanterns flutter from the ceiling.

details, details

The really enjoyable part of styling
any wedding is deciding on all those
wonderful details that can transform a
room, tempt the taste buds and amaze
your guests – the things that transform
the celebration from the so-so to the
sensational. And the good news is that
you don't have to go overboard or spend
a fortune to create a dazzling effect.

details, details

When you began to plan your wedding, you probably gave little thought to the details because finding a venue, booking the honeymoon and choosing a dress seemed much more important. But it is often the details, all those personal touches, that speak volumes and will linger longest in the memory of your guests, so you want to get them just right.

Deciding on the details may be best left until after you have made most of the major decisions – when the venue has been booked, the wedding dress has been chosen, and you are feeling relaxed and confident that plans are progressing and nothing important is going to change.

You are likely to be working with a handful of expert suppliers, so take time at this stage to share your vision in order to benefit from their expertise. They will have been involved in many more weddings than you have, and will have a pretty good idea of what works well and what is less successful. If you know your budget is tight, ask for suggestions on how best to make what you do have go further without compromising on style.

Your aim is to decorate the venue and feed and entertain your guests without overspending or anyone noticing that you may have made a few cost-cutting tweaks along the way. Providing you don't let on that any decision has been made to save money, everyone will presume this is the way your big day has always been planned. For example, getting married on Friday will save you money on venue hire and make negotiating with suppliers easier than if you choose a Saturday, when they can afford to ask top rates. For most of your guests, a Friday wedding is a great way to start the weekend and they'll love your originality.

trade secret

'You want every detail to project your individuality, creating an experience that captures your true essence. This should be tangible from the invitation design right through to your departure at the end of the reception. Your guests' expectations have to be exceeded.'

Aleit Swanepoel,
wedding coordinator

TOP Little touches such as this basket filled with cones of fresh petal confetti are a lovely way to welcome guests to the ceremony.

ABOVE You can even put your stamp on the water bottles by adding your initials to the labels.

OPPOSITE Candlelight never fails to create a romantic mood; this candle-holder has been strategically hung to highlight a decorative orchid-strewn ribbon.

clever cost-cutters (that your guests may not notice)

* have a weekday wedding and forget expensive weekends
* marry outside the traditional wedding season from May to September
* invite fewer guests and avoid the 'plus one' on every invitation
* plan an adults-only day (sorry kids!)
* organize a shorter day; the longer guests are with you, the more they cost
* make your own place cards, menus and table plan on a computer
* open a pay bar during the evening

YOUR WEDDING THEME

Giving your wedding a theme probably sounds a little theatrical but for most couples a theme simply means coordination. The simplest wedding theme is based on colour – choosing a palette that will be used throughout the day, for flowers, accessories and decorative touches such as the napkins on the tables. Themes can be extended into a dress code for guests – for example, specifying black tie for a formal evening reception. A more elaborate theme can be chosen to echo the season or the historical significance of the venue.

If you are contemplating an elaborate theme, it is wise to err on the side of caution unless you are sure that your guests will be happy to wear what amounts to fancy dress. Costume hire is expensive and there is nothing worse than half the guests going along with the theme and the other half turning up in more usual wedding attire.

In the case of a bride or groom who wants to celebrate ethnic background, incorporating cultural elements in the marriage ceremony, in the venue decorations and in the menu is always popular with the other guests, symbolizing the joining of the two families as well as the two cultures.

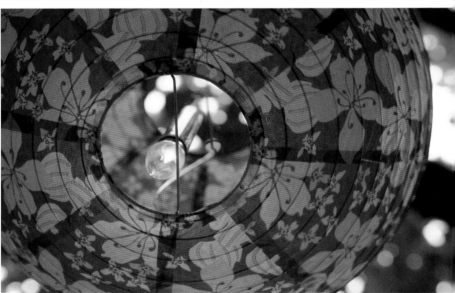

keep guests smiling

* Set up a wedding website with all the relevant details such as directions, local accommodation and gift registry information. You can then post photographs on the site after the wedding for everyone to enjoy.
* Give friends a ring to find out the name of the 'plus one' so you can make invitations feel more personal.
* Keep everyone informed of timings throughout the day. Print timings for the ceremony, drinks reception, sit-down and departure on the invitation.

* If you'll be disappearing for photographs, make sure everyone has a drink and nibbles to keep them going.
* If your seating plan is proving too complicated, consider having a buffet instead so people can seat themselves.
* Plan the dance music carefully to lessen the chances of an empty dance floor. Provide a quiet room for guests who want to chat.
* Evening guests will expect some food, so speak to your caterers about providing a simple but interesting buffet.

TOP While most of your efforts will be concentrated on how the venue looks at eye level, don't forget what's going on above your heads. Here, Chinese paper lanterns have been used to enliven a marquee/tent ceiling.

ABOVE Paper lanterns can also be hung from trees or an outside structure such as a gazebo to transform a patio area into a welcoming space for a dance floor or a drinks reception.

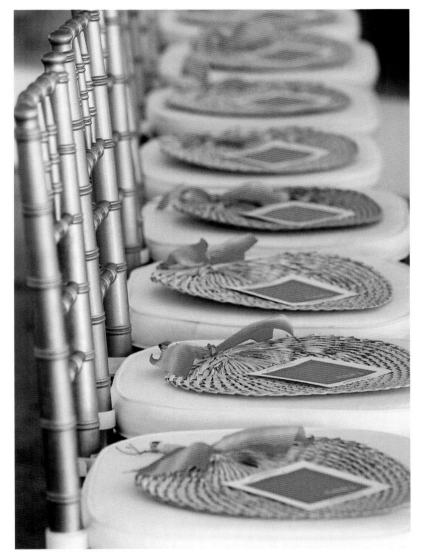

or peonies in full bloom. If possible, eat outdoors either in a marquee/tent with open sides or on long tables under the shade of big white umbrellas.

harvest The colours of autumn are perfect for a rustic country wedding. Choose a barn or vineyard setting and keep the atmosphere relaxed and informal. Serve a seasonal menu with dishes based on Thanksgiving or Guy Fawkes' night, for example.

Christmas Plan your wedding around the festive season – everyone enjoys a double celebration. Decoration is easy; your venue will probably have a Christmas tree already and all you'll have to add is rows of poinsettia plants for colour and piles of glitzy baubles for centrepieces. Serve a traditional menu with goblets of mulled wine.

medieval A castle or historical mansion gives you the chance to be king and queen for the day. Set up the room in banquet style with long rather than round tables and light a roaring fire in the hearth. Entertain guests with a court jester or a magician.

glamour For an adults-only reception, ask guests to dress to impress. Either specify black tie or put 'glamour' on the invitations. Start with cocktails, choose a black-and-white theme, and finish with a jazz band. Set up a casino and give everyone a pile of chips, with a bottle of champagne for whoever wins the most during the evening.

ABOVE The order of service is printed onto coloured card and attached to a raffia fan for each guest to use at a tropically themed wedding – a welcome treat on a hot afternoon.

ABOVE RIGHT You can never be sure what the weather will be like, even during high summer. If there's a chance of a shower, think about providing a few umbrellas (in wedding white, of course) for the use of guests.

successful wedding themes

Easter Choose a spring colour palette of yellow, blue, pink, green and lilac. Decorate tables with baskets of mini-eggs. Serve lamb with fresh spring vegetables. If there are children among the guests, you could organize an Easter egg hunt.

summer White always looks fresh in the sunshine, especially as a background to splashes of bright colour from, say, buckets of old-fashioned roses

trade secret

'Often it's the little things – a fresh flower tucked inside a napkin ribbon, party bags for children or delicious ice cream served with your wedding cake – that set your wedding apart from others and create memories. When the venue, florist and photographer are booked and you've found your dream wedding dress, sit down with a notepad and think about all the inexpensive extras that will delight your guests.'

Catherine Westwood, editor, *Wedding* magazine

delicious and impressive

* Food stations offering dishes from around the world: pizza from Italy, dim sum from China, mini hot dogs and burgers from America, fish and chips from the UK.
* A mixture of fresh seafood served from an ice bar.
* A variety of roast meats from your own carvery, all cut to order by a chef.
* A crêpe station serving a mixture of fresh and savoury crêpes made to order.
* Family-style service with platters of food placed on each table for guests to help themselves.
* A summer picnic with each group of guests getting their own basket filled with sandwiches, mini bottles of bubbly, cheese and tubs of strawberries and cream.

THE WEDDING MENU

Your guests will certainly remember whether or not they enjoyed the food you served at the wedding reception so you need to think carefully about each course in order to serve a well-balanced menu with perhaps a few little surprises to prevent it from being predictable. But, if you want to please most of your guests, the safest option is to choose dishes that are likely to appeal to the majority of tastes – nothing too rich, too highly spiced or too elaborate.

When you first meet your caterers to discuss possible dishes, let them know your personal favourites and also the general age range of the people on your guest list. If your families come from different cultures, it's an attractive idea to reflect this in the menu by theming the courses to celebrate your mixed heritage. Alternatively, you can theme just one course. For example, you could encourage guests to help themselves from a sushi bar for the starter or set up an ice-cream parlour to serve towering sundaes instead of a traditional dessert.

If you are expecting quite a few children to come to the reception, think about offering a child-friendly menu with a couple of healthy(ish) options that will keep both the little ones and their parents happy. Small children are much more likely to enjoy small courses with lots of interesting finger foods than two or three main courses. You also need to make sure that children have something to eat from the moment everyone is seated, even if it's no more than bread sticks and a selection of chopped fruit and vegetables, until the main dishes are served when the adults' food appears.

If you have chosen a strong colour scheme for the day, ask your caterers about reflecting this in some of the dishes. Obviously, you don't want to serve anything that looks unappetizing simply because it suits your theme but there are often clever ways to add colour and keep the food looking, as well as tasting, delicious.

edible ideas that are bound to impress

* ✳ a towering wedding cake
* ✳ a chocolate fountain
* ✳ an ice bar
* ✳ themed food stalls
* ✳ a summer picnic
* ✳ a hog roast
* ✳ a themed cocktail bar

OPPOSITE, LEFT Flowers can be used to add delicious scents and decorative touches. Herbs such as rosemary, with its fresh fragrance, are a lovely choice for decorating napkins.

OPPOSITE, RIGHT For a little extra impact, you can colour-match your table stationery with a flower head as in this pairing of a yellow menu card and a vibrant yellow orchid.

ABOVE Make sure at least one of the dishes on your menu includes the 'ahh' factor. This fruit dessert is made special by the addition of the couple's initials piped in chocolate.

ABOVE RIGHT Allow yourself one extravagance – in this case, a towering five-tier wedding cake in which each tier is separated by masses of fresh red roses.

RECEPTION DRINKS

Apart from the food, alcoholic drinks make up a substantial part of the reception budget. You can buy your drinks direct from the venue or a catering company, or buy from the local off-licence, liquor stores or supermarket and take them with you. If you are thinking of providing your own wine, be warned that most venues will charge you a corkage fee to cover the cost of chilling, uncorking, pouring and serving the wine to your guests. Your cost-effective wine may not be such a bargain after all!

champagne

As a classic celebration drink, champagne is the ideal wedding tipple and your guests will probably want to indulge in at least one glass, even if it's just to toast the couple. To be called champagne, the wine has to come from the Champagne region of France, but there are lots of excellent, reasonably priced alternatives from America, Australia and New Zealand to help stretch your budget.

Ask your caterer or the local wine company for recommendations and spend a weekend or two indulging in a tasting session. The word 'brut' on the label means it is dry, 'demi-sec' is sweet, and 'sec' is the sweetest. Pink champagne is perfect for weddings and comes in a variety of hues from the palest pastel to a deep rose. Serve well chilled in tall flutes to maximize the bubbles or in traditional bowl-shaped champagne glasses for an added touch of glamour.

TOP If you want a stylish but low-key option, a cocktail party is a popular alternative to a sit-down reception.

MIDDLE On a hot day, invest in lots of ice so drinks can be offered from chilled containers decorated with flower heads.

RIGHT If you have a limited budget, consider creating an interesting wedding cocktail and giving it an appropriate name. This can be offered instead of champagne when guests arrive at the reception.

size matters

Impress your guests and serve them champagne from oversize bottles (for this purpose, a bottle contains 750ml).

magnum	2 bottles
jeroboam	4 bottles
rehoboam	6 bottles
methuselah	8 bottles
salmanazar	12 bottles
balthazar	18 bottles
nebuchadnezzar	20 bottles

wine

Regardless of what food you are serving, your guests will expect to be offered a choice of red or white wine with the meal. Find out from the venue what it can offer and don't turn up your nose at the house wines; they are often good and excellent value for money. Choose the wine to suit the season and style of menu. For example, in high summer a chilled chardonnay or rosé will be welcomed by your guests, whereas in winter, when you are likely to be serving hearty fare, a full-bodied red Bordeaux or Merlot will provide a warming treat.

Wine is either served by waiting staff, who offer people a choice as they go around between courses, or a couple of bottles of both red and white wine are put in the centre of each table for guests to serve themselves. Make sure you order enough bottles, allowing for about half a bottle per guest, and expect to get about five glasses out of each one. Most venues will let you buy on a sale-or-return basis, which means you pay only for the bottles that get opened.

cocktails

Cocktail parties are always popular and are a stylish way to welcome guests to the reception. Ask the bartender at your venue to suggest two or three alternatives using the classic gin, vodka and non-alcoholic mixes and then you can give each one a name that is personal to you or the wedding. Just keep an eye on what the venue will be charging you for each cocktail as cocktails tend to be easily consumed and can be pricey. If budget is a big issue, a bowl of punch – suitably named, of course – is the most cost-effective option.

soft drinks

You need to spare a thought for your guests who don't drink alcohol and for those who may be driving. In summer months, in particular, everyone will welcome a glass of something non-alcoholic at some point in the evening. Water and orange juice are the classic offerings but they are a bit dull. How about providing flavoured waters, home-made lemonade and interesting fruit cordials? All can be served from chilled, ice-filled jugs topped with slices of fruit and sprigs of mint.

RIGHT Your venue will probably offer traditional glasses, but for a contemporary wedding you may like to hire some funky glasses to amuse your guests from the moment they arrive.

cool cocktails

Some favourite wedding tipples to delight your guests. The wedding punch makes approximately 5 litres/20 cups.

sealed with a kiss

50 ml/2 oz. chocolate liqueur such as
    Godiva or crème de cacao
35 ml/1.5 oz. vodka
Hershey's Kiss
Pour the chocolate liqueur and vodka into a shaker with ice, shake well, and pour into a chilled cocktail glass. Put a Hershey's Kiss in the bottom for the added love touch.

classic kir royale

champagne
10 ml/½ oz. crème de cassis
Pour the cassis into the bottom of a champagne glass and fill with champagne. Add a raspberry or a slice of strawberry to decorate – and give it a name that's all your own.

classic wedding punch

500 ml/2 cups vodka
1 litre/4 cups unsweetened
    pineapple juice
1 litre/4 cups unsweetened
    cranberry juice
1.5 litres/6 cups ginger ale
450 g/2 cups sugar
Mix all the ingredients together and serve in a large punch bowl with plenty of ice. If you are using sweetened juices, leave out the sugar.

THE WEDDING CAKE

The cake is usually the focal point of any wedding reception and you should think about what sort of cake you would like at the same time as you are considering the food menu. There is a wide range of different options, ranging from a classic tiered cake to a tower of individual cupcakes. To find a cake maker, speak to your caterers, who may have a baker as part of their team. Alternatively, the venue may be able to recommend a favourite supplier or you can find a specialist cake-maker on the internet. Whoever you choose, ask to see their portfolio to get an idea of what they do and then ask to sample some of the cakes. No matter how good your cake looks, it must taste delicious.

what to ask a potential cake-maker

* do you charge per cake or per slice?
* what size cake do I need to feed my guests?
* what is the delivery charge?
* will you come to the venue to set up the cake?
* can you provide a cake stand and knife?

THIS PAGE Whether your wedding is big or small, you will want a wedding cake. These days there are so many tempting options, from miniature fairy cakes to traditional tiers of iced fruit cake. Just remember that it must taste as good as it looks.

OPPOSITE A popular choice is the American stack cake, which has tiers placed directly on top of one another rather than separated by pillars. This simple example is decorated with fresh roses dusted with icing sugar.

trade secret

'The wedding cake is the visual focal point at the reception and will get a great deal of attention throughout the event. It should not only look gorgeous but should taste delicious. I think it is always rather special to reflect the personal taste and individual style of the bride and groom.'

Peggy Porschen, cake designer

An average three-tiered cake will serve up to one hundred guests, but bear in mind that the more complicated you make the design the more expensive the cake will be. If you need to feed a large number of guests, your baker should be able to provide extra slices to keep in the kitchen to serve once the main cake has been cut.

The traditional wedding cake is a rich fruit cake, rather like Christmas cake, with a butter-cream filling and a coating of royal icing. Your baker may use fondant icing if you want a lot of decoration because it gives a nice smooth surface for moulded flowers and piped details.

Fruit cake isn't to everyone's taste, so many couples choose to have their cake made from flavoured sponge. Lemon, orange, carrot and chocolate are all favourites and you can even mix each tier so that there is something for everyone. If you want to keep the top tier for your first child's christening, it needs to be a fruit cake since sponge will not keep in the freezer successfully.

If you are thinking of having an exotically flavoured cake, how about serving it as dessert and thereby cutting your food budget? Once the main course is finished, you will need to hold the cake-cutting ceremony, then the cake can be sliced and served as a pudding. With the addition of cream, ice cream or a fruit sauce, chocolate cake in particular works perfectly.

The cake is usually displayed on a small cake table in a corner of the room where it can easily be admired but is not in danger of being knocked over. Once the cake has been cut, sliced and served to your guests, the venue staff should wrap and re-box any that is left over, which you will need to arrange to be taken home.

ABOVE Position the wedding cake on a table where it can be the focal point of the reception and be enjoyed by all your guests as they eat their meal.

BELOW Fresh flowers can be effective as cake decorations. Work with your florist and the cake-maker to make sure you choose the most suitable flowers; cakes can be heavy and some flowers are easily squashed.

cake styles

traditional tiers The most formal style of cake, consisting of several tiers, in which small pillars are set foursquare to support each tier.

American stack A modern option in which each tier of the cake sits directly on top of one another with no pillars in between.

cupcakes Individual fairy cakes are piled into a tower on a tiered cake stand. If you choose this option, ask your baker to make a small cutting cake so you don't miss out on the cake-cutting ceremony.

croquembouche A French dessert with cream-filled choux-pastry profiteroles piled into a tower and covered in a rich toffee or chocolate sauce and spun sugar.

WEDDING FAVOURS

As part of the traditional setting at a wedding table, guests are greeted with a favour that is both symbolic and acts as a little thank-you gift. Favours are usually five sugared almonds representing health, wealth, fertility, happiness and longevity presented in netting or a small container. At a modern wedding, traditional almonds are replaced with all manner of gifts, ranging from edible favours to lottery tickets. A token gift to say welcome and thanks for coming is an attractive touch but is definitely not expected if your budget doesn't allow.

thoroughly modern favours

* custom-created CD of the couple's favourite songs
* miniature bottles of wine with personalized labels
* lottery tickets
* packets of seeds or potted plants
* unusual Christmas baubles
* bride and groom cookies
* a mini wedding cake
* a charity donation on behalf of each guest

RIGHT A favour is a lovely way to thank guests for joining your celebrations. The item need not be expensive; something that has a personal touch will always be the most appreciated.

LEFT AND BELOW Weddings held in a place unfamiliar to your guests or in a foreign country offer you the chance to enjoy a spectacular setting for a weekend of celebrations. This type of wedding takes a great deal of initial planning but, for a memorable occasion, it is worth all the hard work.

WELCOME PACKS

If you are hosting a destination wedding or have many guests travelling some distance and staying in local accommodation, it's a good idea to provide a welcome pack in their hotel room.

Put together a few items that are useful (a local map, details of restaurants, bank, shops) and a few things that will make your guests smile (sweets/candy, aspirin, a miniature bottle of wine), as well as a postcard from you and your groom thanking them for making the trip and saying how much you are looking forward to seeing them.

If guests will be bringing children, you could also put together a welcome box for each child or group of children, including a few sweet treats, a pack of cards, picture books, colouring pencils and drawing paper.

WEDDING TRANSPORT

You will no doubt want to make a stylish entrance – and exit, if you are having your ceremony and reception at two separate locations – and there is an abundance of transport methods available that do the job and provide perfect photographic opportunities at the same time. If you are having the ceremony and reception at the same venue, then you can making a saving on your budget since none of your guests will be around to witness the big moment as you arrive.

A classic car or limousine is the most popular form of wedding transport, usually in bridal white with the addition of an oversize ribbon on the grille and a floral arrangement in the back window. There are also many specialist vintage car-hire companies offering a range of gorgeous classic cars. For a country wedding, the bride and her father may like to travel to the ceremony in a horse-drawn carriage. If it's practical, you could also think about providing transport for all the guests to and from the wedding and hire a vintage bus.

LEFT Organizing interesting transport to take you to the ceremony will make you feel extra-special as well as offering a great photo opportunity.

BELOW If a large number of guests need to be transported to and from the venue, think about hiring a vintage bus or a fleet of old-style taxis.

ABOVE You can't beat live music to add flavour to any celebration. A classical guitar, a harp or piano player are all suitable options for entertaining guests during the pre-reception drinks party.

ENTERTAINMENT

Entertainment covers just about everything from the musical choices you make for the ceremony to a possible fireworks finale as the two of you leave the reception as husband and wife.

Music is the soundtrack to your wedding day so you will want it to be just right. Think about the important moments during the day when music would be appropriate – for example, as you walk down the aisle; during the ceremony and to entertain your guests while you are signing the register; at the reception during cocktails; during the meal; then, of course, to entertain your guests throughout the evening. Don't feel that you need to have live music throughout the day; this would be expensive and really isn't necessary.

Recommendations from friends can help you to find the best entertainers but, once you have made a shortlist, it is important that you hear them play, live if possible. Don't rely on someone else's opinion. You are looking for music that will suit the tastes of all your guests, so a middle-of-the-road route is usually the safest option. There is nothing worse than an empty dance floor or your older relatives wanting to leave early because they don't enjoy loud music. Most wedding bands and DJs have a favoured play-list, so make sure you look through this and delete any songs you hate.

Music isn't the only way of entertaining your guests at the reception. There are lots of mime artists, magicians, celebrity lookalikes and caricaturists who can walk around as your guests eat, entertaining each table. It all depends on the amount of entertainment you want to provide and, of course, your budget.

entertaining suggestions
an afternoon drinks reception for 50 guests
A singer or group who is capable of performing a variety of ballads. A close-up magician moving around the room entertaining groups of three or four people.

a reception with lots of children
A crèche in a separate room is always a good idea, particularly if there is a large number of children under-six. Qualified childminders will provide a variety of activities from colouring to puzzles. Older children can enjoy the party from a child-only table with their own menu and pens and paper to keep them occupied. In good weather, a treasure hunt always goes down well.

an intimate reception with fewer than 50 guests
A string quartet or jazz trio with an easy-listening style that is not too intrusive on the conversation. A silhouette cutter or caricaturist will have everyone captured on paper before the end of the evening.

a formal reception with more than 150 guests
A classic five-piece band with an optional singer to entertain guests during the meal and to provide music for dancing during the evening. Later in the evening, set up a James Bond-style casino. Specialist companies provide all the equipment and the staff although real money doesn't change hands.

ABOVE What better way to end the day than with a spectacular fireworks display? Ten minutes of pyrotechnics will send your guests home with a smile.

BELOW You could invest in a dance lesson or two before the wedding so you can impress everyone with your nimble moves when you take to the floor.

first-dance favourites
Can You Feel the Love Tonight?	*Elton John*
Endless Love	*Diana Ross/Lionel Richie*
Fly Me to the Moon	*Frank Sinatra*
Forever	*Nat King Cole*
How Sweet It Is	*James Taylor*
My Girl	*The Temptations*
Only You	*The Platters*
The Greatest Love of All	*Whitney Houston*

WEDDING PHOTOGRAPHY

Since you have gone to all this effort to create a beautiful day, you want to make sure that it is captured for posterity to revisit and enjoy for many years to come. It is little wonder that a wedding album becomes a family treasure.

Professional photographers are expensive, but brides who scrimp on this are nearly always disappointed. Yes, it does cost a lot – but you can't go back and do it all again if the photographs are out of focus. Trust a professional rather than a talented friend; you get what you pay for and this is one area where you shouldn't compromise.

You may think that finding a photographer is rather low on your 'to do' list, but popular wedding photographers get booked up quickly, so it is important to start looking as early as possible. Decide on the type of pictures you prefer. Do you want traditional shots or a more relaxed style? Do you want everything in colour or a mixture of black and white and colour? For many couples, having an engagement portrait is a good way of testing the skill of a potential photographer and whether you like him or her. You should also ask to see whole albums, not just a carefully compiled portfolio of the best shots from several weddings. You want to make sure that the standard will remain consistent throughout the day.

Ask about packages and what's included. How much are extra prints or CDs? How much will the photographer charge to stay all day rather than just cover the ceremony and the start of the reception?

BELOW Even if you love colour photography, don't dismiss the old-fashioned elegance that black and white prints can offer. A mixture of the two styles is usually recommended for the most memorable album.

trade secret

'Review at least two weddings from start to finish, then consider some questions. Do you feel that you were there? Were you moved by the pictures? Was the presentation and print quality to the standard that you are happy with? Is the style of the photography you are shown exactly what you want for your album? If not, choose another photographer.'

Julie Lovegrove, wedding photographer

styles of photography

traditional There is a lot to be said for traditional and shamelessly romantic shots, as long as they are not clichéd and the quality is excellent.

reportage This candid style of photography, where the photographer captures impromptu moments as well as more formal shots, creates a storybook feel. From the bride getting ready with her bridesmaids to the best man sneakily practising his speech behind the marquee/tent, you will end up with a true flavour of the whole day.

black and white Even if you love colour and want the world to see how much effort you have put into the decorations, it is still a good idea to include a few black-and-white shots. With the ability to throw atmospheric contrasts of light and dark, the overall effect can be very stylish and flattering.

sepia Sepia photographs consist of instantly recognisable brownish shots, reminiscent of very early photographic styles. White dresses appear ivory and the soft tones are usually very flattering.

hand-tinting This is a special technique applied to black-and-white prints where the photographer adds splashes of colour; for example, only the bouquet is in colour in a black-and-white shot.

digital images Many photographers these days will use a digital camera. Computer techniques allow for the removal of blemishes and 'red eye', the bride and groom can be superimposed on to a different location and the sky turned an amazing shade of blue – whatever your heart desires.

RIGHT Great wedding photographs don't happen just by chance. Ideally, you should commission a photographer who has worked at your venue before or at least can let you see you an album of images that show creativity and imagination.

must-have wedding photographs

* the bride and bridesmaids getting ready
* the bridal bouquet
* the bride and her father leaving for the ceremony
* the groom and best man getting ready
* the wedding rings on a cushion or prayer book
* the wedding transport
* the bride walking down the aisle
* the ceremony
* signing the register
* the first married kiss
* the bride and groom and family outside the ceremony
* the couple and the main bridal party
* the couple and both sets of parents
* the couple with all their guests (if room allows)
* the reception venue before the guests arrive
* close-up details of the tables, favours, menu cards, etc.
* the wedding cake
* the couple cutting the cake
* the first dance as man and wife
* tossing the bouquet
* the couple leaving at the end of the reception

THE VIDEOGRAPHER

If you want to commission a video of your wedding, you may well choose a videographer who works at the same studio as the photographer. Or your photographer can probably recommend someone he or she has worked with in the past. It is important that the two of them have a good working rapport since you don't want them getting in each other's way.

Ask to see samples of the cameraman's work. Again, you want to see a video of a wedding, not just carefully edited highlights from several weddings. You will be paying as much for the post-production (that is, the work done in the studio after the wedding) as for the footage shot on the day. The addition of background music, special effects such as slow motion and captions can make your video look more like a feature film than a home movie.

trade secret

'Don't forget to consider the photographer's approach. If you are uncomfortable in front of the camera, hire a photojournalist who will unobtrusively capture the day as it unfolds. If you prefer a more hands-on approach, work with a traditional photographer who will pose you throughout the day. Whatever approach you choose, just make sure it fits with the way you envisage your perfect wedding day!'

Rodney Bailey, wedding photojournalist

THE RECEPTION TIMETABLE

Every wedding is different, but this will give you an idea of the running order at a traditional reception that includes dinner and dancing.

4.00pm arrive at the reception

The wedding party arrives at the reception followed by the guests.

4.00–4.30pm the receiving line

The bride, groom and main wedding party form a receiving line and greet guests one by one. A lot of couples choose not to have a receiving line, feeling it is too formal and time-consuming.

4.30–5.30pm cocktails

Guests enjoy a drink, canapés and check the table plan for where they will be sitting. A string quartet or a harpist could provide music or you could put on a classical music CD to provide background music. The bride and groom are usually absent at this point having photographs taken.

5.45pm announcements

Dinner is announced by a toastmaster or head waiter and guests start to move into the dining area to find their seats. It is usual for both sets of parents, the best man and bridesmaids to go in first, followed by other guests. The bride and groom are announced and guests stand as they come into the room.

6.00pm welcome

Once everyone is seated and the room is quiet, the bride's father or a toastmaster welcomes everyone to the wedding. A minister may say a blessing.

6.15pm dinner is served

The first course is served to the top table, then all the other guests. Other courses follow in steady, but not rushed, succession.

7.45pm toasts

After dessert, glasses are refilled and the bride's father toasts the health of the bride and groom.

7.50 pm speeches

The father of the bride makes the first speech and is followed by the groom, who responds on behalf of himself and his new wife. The groom proposes a toast to the bridesmaids and may also give out a small thank-you present to the bridesmaids. The best man replies on behalf of the bridesmaids and then makes his speech. If the bride wants to say a few words, she can do this at the same time or just after her husband.

8.30 pm cutting the cake

The bride and groom cut the wedding cake, which is then taken away and cut into neat pieces to serve with coffee. Any evening-only guests will usually be invited to arrive just after the cake has been cut and should be welcomed with a drink.

8.45 pm the first dance

Tables are cleared to make way for dancing or guests move into another room for the second part of the evening. The bride and groom take the floor for their chosen first-dance tune. The next dance is for the bride and her father and the groom and his mother. Other guests gradually take to the floor after the first couple of minutes.

ABOVE Ladies don't always want to wear large hats while eating and dancing so provide a line with pegs and create an eye-catching display.

RIGHT Many guests appreciate soft drinks, tea and coffee being available through the day.

FAR RIGHT Make your exit as dramatic as your entrance by lining the venue driveway with fireworks such as these Roman candles, set to go off just as the bridal car leaves the reception.

Depending on the venue, the evening will draw to a close at a set time or may go on until dawn. If you do anticipate partying into the night, remember to make it clear to your guests that you won't be leaving. It's traditional for guests to wait until after the bride and groom leave before departing themselves, and older friends and those with small children will want to go home.

At an agreed time before too many guests have left, it is fun to indulge in that age-old tradition of tossing the bouquet. All the single girls crowd around the bride, who faces away and tosses her bouquet backwards. Whoever catches it will be the next to marry.

If you are going to leave the party before your guests, you can either slip away to change or leave in your wedding outfits to go to the hotel where you will spend your first night. Many couples like to make a dramatic exit and a short firework display is now a popular way to bring the wedding to a close.

Yolande Naude and James Pietersen

my wedding style

Nothing demonstrates the beauty of a
stylish wedding than seeing examples
of real celebrations. On the following
pages there are six very different
weddings for you to enjoy, chosen to
demonstrate the flair of individual style.
Each featured couple has successfully
created a magical day full of inspirational
touches and personal style in locations as
varied as the English countryside and a
deserted beach in Zanzibar.

English picnic

INFORMALITY * CHAMPAGNE AND CUPCAKES
VINTAGE COLOUR PALETTE * EASTER EGGS * DRAGONFLIES

Katie Joyce and Alan Whysall wanted a wedding with an informal atmosphere, so they chose a picnic followed by dinner at a small modern hotel with a reputation for excellent food. The whole day had a non-traditional feel: there were no bridesmaids, no speeches – not even a 'real' wedding cake. 'We chose primary colours to reflect the spring-like qualities of the April afternoon, with touches of vintage creams and browns to match our outfits,' says Katie. 'All the beautiful flowers were arranged by my green-fingered mother. She made the bouquet using my favourite flowers – parrot tulips, hyacinths, hydrangea flowers, roses and pussy willow – and also arranged all the reception flowers. She collected vintage glass dishes from antiques fairs

and planted them with white hyacinths. All the guests commented on the amazing fragrance.

'After the garden ceremony, our guests enjoyed mini bottles of champagne and cupcakes laid out on picnic tables under the trees, where we were joined by a peacock. Since the wedding took place just before Easter, we decorated the reception with vintage glass bowls filled with mini chocolate eggs that added spots of bright colour around the room.'

'For dinner we served antipasti followed by chargrilled chicken breast; dessert was girls/boys puddings of crème brulée and plum frangipani tart – and swapping was encouraged! Our wedding "cake" was made of artistically arranged local cheeses and was absolutely delicious.'

South African romance

AFRICAN SAILING BOATS * WHITE DRESS CODE
NAUTICAL BLUE AND WHITE * BEACH BONFIRES

Yolande Naude married James Pietersen in the ruins of an Anglican church on Zanzibar island. 'It was pure magic,' says Yolande. 'We then took African sailing boats, or dhows, to the reception, which was held on the beach at Mtoni Marine. I run a travel company called Dream Destinations, which specializes in honeymoons, so you could say that romance is my business. We had both fallen in love with Zanzibar on a previous trip, so when we decided to get married, the choice of location was easy. We wanted our guests to have a holiday at the same time as celebrating our wedding. There are no florists on the island, but we reckoned that candles and beach bonfires would be much more effective than flower arrangements for this type of wedding. We chose a nautical theme in relaxed island style with a colour scheme of navy blue, white and a dash of red; all the guests wore white. Everyone was given a red fan with white tassles and James wrote a poem that was printed in white inside.'

'The day's high point was the simultaneous arrival at the beach of the three dhows, with the thundering sounds of the African drums as we disembarked and walked towards a long table on the beach . . . the surprise and delight on the faces of our family and friends made it an unforgettable moment for us both.'

lanterns in the park

CHINESE LANTERNS * CANDLELIGHT * ORGANIC MATERIALS * LOVE LETTERS * HORA DANCE

For their Californian wedding, Jennifer Gormley and Jonathan Klein chose their favourite colours of orange and lavender and used them on everything from the flowers to the Chinese lanterns in the trees. 'The ceremony was held at dusk under a beautiful magnolia tree, illuminated by the lanterns and paper bags containing votives. It looked fantastic. I wanted an organic feel to the day and giant pumpkins were placed around the venue. My bouquet was a mixture of dahlias, succulents, hydrangea, bark and roses. We didn't want traditional centrepieces so used bark, decorated with crab apples, moss and persimmons.

We also included family photos dating back several generations. Guests dined on salads, grilled chicken with lemon and vegetables. Instead of a cake, there was a choice of chocolate, vanilla or coconut cupcakes. Our memorable moment was the ceremony. We wanted it to feel personal so wrote our own vows – more like love letters to one another. My grandfather wrote a poem, ending it with an acknowledgement to my grandmother who passed away the year before. Not a dry eye in the house. The second memorable moment was the Jewish Hora dance. Being raised up on a chair with 200 people around us was exhilarating!'

red and white weekend

TWO-DAY PARTY * WHITE UMBRELLAS * HEART ILLUMINATIONS * BRILLIANT SPLASHES OF COLOUR

Dorine Berger and Stephane Reinstein's wedding was supposed to be a weekend of relaxation and laughter in the South African sunshine and although they all had an amazing time, it poured with rain. 'Our young daughter running riot and pulling down the flowers is probably what people remember the most! Luckily we had invested in a selection of large white umbrellas, which came in very handy and everyone said that huddling in front of the open fires to warm up definitely added to the intimacy of the occasion. We held our party over two days with most of our guests staying overnight at the venue, Clouds Guesthouse in Stellenbosch, and having a little holiday as well as celebrating with us.'

'Our colour scheme was dramatic red and white with hearts playing a central role in the decorations. The dining area was illuminated by several hearts that twinkled in the background and looked so pretty as it got dark. Our table flowers were an informal mix of white orchids, red roses, eucalyptus, melkbos and stephanotis displayed in small and tall containers. We chose red linens and red wine glasses that added a splash of colour to the room. The menu was a starter of angel's hair pasta with chilli and prawns. Next, guests could roll-their-own pancakes with crispy hoisin duck. The main dish was a stack of beef fillet medallions or seared oriental salmon and dessert was a liquid-centered chocolate pudding.'

among the vines

SUNSHINE * CALIFORNIAN WINE * FALL COLOURS * FAIRY LIGHTS * FIRST KISS

Kristen Klapproth and Ikaika Fitzsimmons held their September wedding at the spectacular Sebastiani Vineyards in Sonoma. 'The ceremony was outside and conducted by Pastor Mike who travelled from Ikaika's childhood home in Hawaii. The reception was in the antique barrel room that was strung with brilliant fairy lights to welcome guests on arrival. Our colour scheme was purple and violet mixed with sage green that perfectly suited the season. Flowers were important and we chose white calla lilies, roses, green and white hydrangea and purple lisianthus. For the reception tables we used low cylinders covered in ribbon and mounded with green hydrangeas and lisianthus. The wine barrels were trimmed with a eucalyptus garland with hydrangeas and roses. My bouquet was white roses and miniature calla lilies.'

'The menu was a Tuscan salad and goat's cheese followed by a choice of pork tenderloin, grilled chicken or Portobello Mushroom Napoleon. For dessert we had a buffet of chocolate walnut squares, blondies with white chocolate and macadamia nuts and a seasonal fruit bar. The wedding cake was filled with Champagne custard, covered with butter cream frosting and decorated with ribbon, grapes and roses. Probably my most memorable moment was our first kiss as husband and wife.'

festive iridescence

JEWEL COLOURS * WHITE DOVES * ASIAN FLOWERS
FOOD STATIONS * LAUGHTER AND FUN

Laura Echols and Drew Pollard chose deep iridescent jewel tones to give their wedding day in Virginia a subtly Asian look. 'These colours are used throughout our home and we wanted our wedding to be a reflection of the style we both love,' explains Laura. 'During the ceremony our pastor spoke about the seven aspects of love, and to symbolize this we released seven white doves at the moment we became husband and wife.'

'The reception ballroom was separated into two areas by swathes of orange and pink fabric, one area for dining and one for dancing. Guests helped themselves from food stations serving dishes such as sushi, crab claws, salads and pasta. There was also a "chill-out room" with comfy sofas and a cocktail bar. A branch of Asian manzanita blossom was the "logo" we used on everything from the save-the-date cards and the invitations to lining the aisle and decorating the reception tables. We created a "Christmas tree" from large manzanita branches and covered this with jewel-coloured baubles onto which guests could write messages of good luck throughout the evening. We both love Christmas and these decorations will come out every year to remind us of what a wonderful day we enjoyed.'

the stylist's secret address book

UK SUPPLIERS

GENERAL WEDDING SUPPLIES

Celebrations Plus
www.celebrationsplus.co.uk

Online Wedding Shop
www.onlinewedding
shop.co.uk

CAKES & COOKIES

Cake Modern
www.cakemodern.com

The Cake Shop
www.the-cakeshop.co.uk

Choccywoccydoodah
www.choccywoccydoodah.com

Hummingbird Bakery
www.hummingbirdbakery.com

Konditor & Cook
www.konditorandcook.com

The Little Venice Cake Company
www.lvcc.co.uk

Peggy Porschen
www.peggyporschen.com

Rachel Mount Cakes
www.rachelmount.com

Savoir Design
www.savoirdesign.com

CHAIR COVERS & LINENS

Elite Weddings
www.eliteweddings.co.uk

Nationwide Chair Cover Hire Co
www.chaircovers.org.uk

Northfields
www.linenforhire.com

DANCE LESSONS

First Dance UK
www.firstdanceuk.co.uk

The First Dance
www.the-first-dance.co.uk

FAVOURS & LABELS

Treasured Favours
www.treasuredfavours.co.uk

Sweetie Bag
www.sweetiebag.com

Wedding Paraphernalia
www.wedding
paraphernalia.co.uk

World of Wedding Favours
www.world-of-wedding-
favours.com

HIRE COMPANIES (FURNITURE, CANDELABRA, GLASSES, PROPS)

Jones Catering Equipment Hire
www.joneshire.co.uk

Rayners Hire
www.rayners.co.uk

Spaceworks
www.spaceworks.co.uk

Theme Traders
www.themetraders.com

Top Table Hire
www.toptablehire.com

PHOTOGRAPHY

British Institute of Professional Photography
www.bipp.com

Master Photographers Association
www.thempa.com

RIBBONS & TRIMMINGS

Josyrose
www.josyrose.com

VV Rouleaux
www.vvroutleaux.com

STATIONERY & PAPERWORK

Chartula
www.chartula.co.uk

Smythson of Bond Street
www.smythson.com

Susan O'Hanlon
www.susanohanlon.com

Xoxo Weddings
www.xoxo-weddings.co.uk

WEDDING PLANNERS & STYLISTS

Deborah Dwek
www.deborahdwek
weddings.co.uk

Kathryn Lloyd
www.kathrynlloyd.co.uk

Siobhan Craven Robins
www.siobhancraven-
robins.co.uk

Wedding Bible Events
www.weddingbible.co.uk

WEDDING IDEAS

Balloon Lady
www.balloonlady.co.uk

Chocolate Fountain
www.chocolatefountain.co.uk

Classic Doves
www.classicdoves.co.uk

The Ice Box
www.theicebox.com

The White Dove Company
www.thewhitedove
company.co.uk

White Canvas Tents
www.whitecanvastents.com

US AND CANADIAN SUPPLIERS

GENERAL WEDDING SUPPLIES

Bliss Weddings Market
www.blissweddings
market.com

Bride Stuff
www.bridestuff.com

Confetti
www.confetti.com

The Knot
www.theknot.com

Wedding Channel
www.weddingchannel.com

Wedding Things
www.weddingthings.com

Wedding Star
www.weddingstar.com

CAKES & COOKIES

Sylvia Weinstock
www.sylviaweinstock.com

DANCE LESSONS

New York Wedding Dance
www.nyweddingdance.com

Waltz Through Life
www.waltzthroughlife.com

FAVOURS & LABELS
Arizona Sweets
www.arizonasweets.com

Beaucoup Favors
www.beau-coup.com

My Wedding Labels
www.myownlabels.com/weddi
ngs.asp

Paper, Ribbon, Wrap
www.paperribbonandwrap.co
m

R&R Personalizing
www.randrpersonalizing.com

HIRE COMPANIES (FURNITURE, CANDELABRA, GLASSES, PROPS)

BBJ Linen
www.bbjlinen.com

Wildflower Linens
www.wildflowerlinens.com

Wedding Linens
www.weddinglinens.com

PHOTOGRAPHY

Society of Wedding & Portrait Photographers
www.swpp.co.uk

Professional Photographers of America
www.ppa.com

STATIONERY & PAPERWORK

Bella Invitations
www.bellainvites.com

Created by Fate
www.cratedbyfate.com

Inviting Smiles
www.invitingsmiles.com

Picture Me Perfect
www.picturemeperfect.com

Stephannie Barba
www.stephanniebarba.com

WEDDING PLANNERS & STYLISTS

Karen Bussen
www.karenbussen.com

Love Luck & Angels
www.loveluckandangelscom

Preston Bailey
www.prestonbailey.com

WEDDING IDEAS

Bentley Meeker Lighting
www.bentleymeeker.com

Brownie Pops
www.browniepops.com

Candy Direct
www.candydirect.com

Chocolat Élégant
www.chocolatelegant.com

Custom Playing Cards
www.customplayingcards.com

Cocktail Umbrellas
www.cocktailumbrellas.com

Chocolate Picture People
www.chocolatepicture
people.com

LA Ice Art
www.laiceart.com

My Jones Soda Company
www.myjones.com

My Own Labels
www.myownlabels.com

Something New Compositions
www.sncomposition.com

NYC Photobooth Hire
www.nycphotobooth.com

OTHER

WEDDING PLANNERS & STYLISTS

Aleit
www.aleit.co.za

Anthony de Col
www.weddingsbystagingconne
tions.com.au

index

credits & acknowledgements

PICTURE CREDITS

Key: ph= photographer, a=above, b=below, r=right, l=left, c=centre.

All photographs © Rodney Bailey (www.rodneybailey.com) unless otherwise stated below:

Page 1 © ph Jean Pierre Uys (www.jeanpierrephotography.co.za); 6 © English Heritage; 7 © Julie Mikos; 16a © ph Tommy Colbert (www.tommycolbert.com); 18 & 20 © ph Julie Mikos; (www.juliemikos.com); 21 © ph Roy Llera (www.royllera.com); 22b, 25cl, & 25br ph Polly Wreford; 28 © ph Julie Mikos; 32-33 main © English Heritage (www.english-heritage.org.uk); 34a © ph Jean Pierre Uys; 34-35b © English Heritage; 36-37 main © English Heritage; 37br © English Heritage; 39 © English Heritage; 42-43a © English Heritage; 42-43b © Crescent Moon (www.crescent-moon.co.uk); 45 © English Heritage; 46 © Confetti (www.confetti.co.uk); 50 ph Claire Richardson; 60b © ph Roy Llera; 62-63, 64 both, 65a © Chartula (www.chartula.co.uk); 65bl ph Carolyn Barber; 66a&c © Chartula; 67bl ph Caroline Arber/designed and made by Jane Cassini and Ann Brownfield; 70 & 71b handwritten stationery © Stephannie Barba (www.stephanniebarba.com); 71a ph Polly Wreford; 73 magnets from Confetti; 88a ph Polly Wreford; 88b & 89br © ph Jean Pierre Uys; 89bl ph Polly Wreford; 90br © ph David Wolfe (www.davidwolfephotography.com); 93ar ph Craig Fordham; 93br ph Polly Wreford; 94cl ph Craig Fordham; 94ar ph Carolyn Barber; 94cl & 95b ph Craig Fordham; 98a ph Craig Fordham; 103 ph Polly Wreford; 104b © ph Jean Pierre Uys; 113b all ph Polly Wreford; 115 all ph Polly Wreford; 120-121 ph Polly Wreford; 125l © ph David Wolfe; 126l ph Polly Wreford; 128b, 129 & 130 © ph Jean Pierre Uys; 133b both © ph Lovegrove Photography (www.lovegroveweddings.com); 134c © ph Jean Pierre Uys; 144-145 © ph Rachel Barnes; 146-147 © ph Jean Pierre Uys; 148-149 © ph Julie Mikos; 152-153 © ph Julie Mikos.

TRADE SECRETS

Many thanks to all the experts who provided their invaluable advice in our exclusive Trade Secret panels throughout the book.

Preston Bailey
www.prestonbailey.com
Rodney Bailey
www.rodneybailey.com
Anthony del Col
www.stagingconnections.com
Stephannie Barba
www.stephanniebarba.com
Deborah Dwek
www.deborahdwekweddings.co.uk
Kathryn Lloyd
www.kathrynlloyd.co.uk
Jo Gartin
www.loveluckandangels.com
Vanessa Gore
www.youandyourwedding.co.uk

Colette Harris
www.youandyourwedding.co.uk
Sarah Haywood
www.weddingbible.co.uk
Charlotte Hewson
www.chartula.co.uk
Charles Howard
www.jalapenolondon.co.uk
Julie Lovegrove
www.lovegroveweddings.com
Bentley Meeker
www.bentleymeeker.com
James Partridge
www.claridges.co.uk
Paula Pryke
www.paula-pryke-flowers.com
Peggy Porschen
www.peggyporschen.co.uk
Kate Smallwood
www.weddingmagazine.co.uk
Aleit Swanepoel
www.aleit.co.za
Nikki Tibbles
www.wildatheart.com
Vera Wang
www.verawang.com
Sylvia Weinstock
www.sylviaweinstock.com
Catherine Westwood
www.weddingmagazine.co.uk